Edge of the Blue

Darry Fraser

This book is a work of fiction. The names, characters, places, and incidents are products of the writer's imagination or have been used fictitiously and are not to be construed as real. Any resemblance to persons, living or dead, actual events, locale organizations is entirely coincidental.

Copyright © 2019 Darry Fraser

All rights reserved.

ISBN: 978-0-9875148-2-0

Acknowledgements

Tony and Phyll Bartram and the teams at Kangaroo Island / Victor Harbor Dolphin Watch, also Phyll for the great dolphin pic. Kangaroo Island Marine Adventures. Susi Parslow for her eagle eye and her red pen. Alice Teasdale at Big Quince Print for the fab cover and for her brainstorming. The community of Kangaroo Island. The do-ers behind the scenes: the volunteers. The conscientious experts, the warriors, the worriers, and those who speak up for positive change in a positive way – citizen scientists.

One

Jed Deveraux heard the silence in the room. Heard his heartbeat thud, felt the dull thumps between his ears. Across the room the city people stared back and he knew their silence was for him. He knew they waited for whatever it was he was about to impart.

Or explode ... With rage.

Keep it together. Keep it together. Wouldn't do to look like a lunatic in front of these academics from the university. Wouldn't do to look like someone with passion and empathy for the sentient beings he and his team represented. Wouldn't do to look like someone *without* a nod for the funds required for research and development, the *real* world stuff. Wouldn't do at all.

He almost snorted aloud.

Wouldn't do to claim his long list of credentials in academia in his own field. Not to mention his upbringing. Nor bore them to death with, according to them, whimsical arguments fuelled by fire in the belly and not much else. Been done before, and fell on deaf ears, their eyes clicking over the dollar signs like one-arm bandit machines.

Keep it together. Keep it together.

Focus. Three things. Focus.

One. Product. He dropped his gaze and stared at Berta Mathieson's plate of lamingtons, a great plate of big sponge squares, thickly coated with Berta's double ooze chocolate icing and rolled in desiccated coconut. Her husband, Tomas did the rolling coconut bit, and thought he was pretty good at it. The plate sat in the middle of the boardroom table.

Drumming his fingers lightly, imperceptibly, on the polished red-gum tabletop, Jed noted that others at the meeting were also mindful of the cakes in the middle of the table.

Two. Provenance. That's how his mother had taught him to do it: roll neat squares of sponge (or vanilla butter cake—package mix if you couldn't be bothered with the real deal) in chocolate icing then in coconut. Lamingtons fixed everything, she'd said. *The magic of lamingtons*. He'd never bought it, especially not when he'd had to stare at her black eye.

Clearly, Berta thought today's problem could be fixed by the magic of lamingtons. The warm and fuzzy hospitality of lamingtons. Who'd have thought? An Aussie icon present at every school fete, bakery and now, in boardrooms across the country. Or maybe only on Australis Island and in his boardroom.

Three. Construction. Stacked into a squat looking tower, seven or eight cakes made up the base tier and then they piled high, layer upon layer until only one sat on top looking like the odd man out instead of king-of-the-castle.

Jed stopped drumming, laced his fingers and rested his hands on the table as he leaned forward. He was calm, focused. Controlled. Composed, his mother had called it. Composure was something else she'd tried to teach him but he'd never fully grasped the concept, not like she had, at the back of someone else's hand.

And grasping the concept wasn't going to start now.

'Jed.' Flynn Lockett caught his eye. 'Go for it.' He angled his head—his burnished auburn hair was now close cropped—at the others across the table.

Flynn, on his right, was tackling the draft Environmental Impact Statement from the mob who wanted to dredge a deep-sea port in Jones Bay on the north coast of the island. That mob wanted to log the island's blue gums and export the timber—right over pristine waters. *Jeez, talk about tackle the big jobs all at once.*

Then Jed glanced over the table at the two men and the one woman who sat opposite him. One of the men, Jim du Pont, was suited and slick, tanned most probably from a bottle—the sun never made you that orange colour. At about sixty, he looked a little bit comfortable, a little bit on the *sitting-on-my-laurels* type, the bloke from R&D. The other, Steve McKay, *Professor* Steve

McKay no less, also around sixty, at a guess. Used to be a field man before the lure of the big bucks won him over and land-locked him in more ways than one.

Both men eyed him. Casual, confident, playing the game. Big city predators waiting to pick off the dumb-arse country hick surfer boy.

I don't think.

He straightened in his seat, flexed his hands again. He brought his gaze up to meet that of the third person.

Roxie Lockett, Flynn's younger sister. She had a pile of folders stacked in front of her, the sort you recycled when you emptied them of stuff you'd forgotten you'd filed there in the first place. Manilla folders. She met his gaze. No emotion. No heat, except for a frown of concentration, or so he thought. But heat would have been there. He remembered her temper when they were kids; it reflected in her wild, red hair, and the fine, scowling brow above her chestnut eyes.

He scowled back at her and shifted his gaze to the lamingtons again. Berta had done well.

Jim du Pont reached for the top square and plonked it down on the paper plate Evie had provided each table setting. Evie, Jed's 2IC, his go-to person, hadn't held back, *no-sir*. Everyone had a paper plate *and* a piece of paper towel to dab away any crumbs. *No holding back.*

'Jed,' Flynn urged again.

Jed took a deep breath. 'Jim. Steve.' He shoved his hair behind his ears with both hands. Old habit to get the wiry thatch off his face. 'We've sat here and listened to your intentions for the last…what—twenty minutes?' He looked at Evie for her confirmation nod then leaned back, comfortable and calm. 'I know—sorry, *we* know research and funding go hand in hand. We *know* that without big dollars we can't save our animals. We know that without a bi-partisan approach our dolphins and whales and other marine life will bear the brunt of,' he paused, 'our current ignorance.' He wanted to say, "*your* current ignorance", but in the spirit of whatever-the-fuck-it-was-called, he refrained. *It's a good speech so far, why ruin it?* So far, he was keeping it under control. 'We also know that our longitudinal photographic identification process here, in Australis Island waters, is non-invasive and has no impact on our animals.' He waited a moment. 'As opposed to the invasive impact of your biopsy darting.'

Du Pont smiled. He had pointy teeth. How do you get pointy teeth? Not all of them were pointy, but enough to notice in his top set, anyway. He tilted forward, clasping his hands on the table, a mimic of Jed's.

'Jed, for God's sake, we agree with you. But biopsy darting is the quickest, cheapest way of gaining the data we need to back our research. We can deliver to your Australis Island Dolphin Watch—and your animals—much better protections if we have the information sooner rather than later.' He kept on smiling, which was distracting.

Exactly how many pointy teeth did he have? He looked like a great white. Big mouth, cold eyes, wary. Expecting dinner. Jed didn't mean to glance at the stand of cakes again, but he did.

Focus. Calm.

Steve McKay nodded with du Pont. 'You were there at my lectures, Jed. You know that the best way to procure information is to dart the animals.' He wiped a hand across his face, pinched his nose, sniffed. 'You know they don't feel a thing.'

Roxie Lockett flinched but Jed barely registered that. He glared at McKay. 'I don't know any such bloody thing.' He dropped his chin. 'You don't reckon you'd feel a dart the size of my little finger ripping into your guts? You reckon you wouldn't feel it scoping out a five mil by forty mil section and sucking it back out of your body?'

Du Pont sat back, glanced at Steve McKay, who shook his head. 'You always were one of my more em*pathetic* students.' The sarcasm wasn't lost on Jed. 'All fired up about the rights of the animal ahead of the benefits of the research.' His smile turned grim. 'No reality, though. If we nab a big find the research dollars will pop out of nowhere in their millions.' He edged forward, pushed the tray of lamingtons out of his way. 'This is going to help the mammals, Jed. Help their future. A little pain now—'

'So, it is painful.'

'—is worth the gain later. See reason.'

'This isn't reason. This is invasive, ignorant and at best, lazy. We have the team here to—'

'You have a team but no funding,' Du Pont interjected.

Jed thought maybe the laurels du Pont sat on were getting prickly. He pressed on, holding his temper. The struggle continued. 'We have a team willing to do the work. We have volunteers, donations.'

'For how much longer?' McKay draped his arm over the back of Roxie Lockett's chair.

Jed squinted at that. *What the fuck—*

Roxie moved in her seat, ignoring McKay, focusing on Jed. 'You know I took the job for—'

'I know what you *thought* you took the job for.' Jed's gaze bored into hers.

Her mouth thinned. 'I took the job because I knew I could assist with this process.'

'What process?' Jed waved his hand around the room. 'This? This isn't a process, this is a railroad. A process brings us all to the table.'

'We're all here now,' Roxie cut in, dark eyes flashing.

'Not in an official capacity,' Jed threw back at her. He stabbed a finger at du Pont and McKay in turn. 'And we'll fight you every inch of the way.'

'You do that, Jed,' du Pont said and stood up. 'But nothing is going to come between my lab and those funding dollars. Nothing.

If it means your dolphins sacrifice some blubber for the greater good, so be it.'

Jed shoved to his feet, his chair thrust back and crashing to the wall behind him. 'And who bloody gives you permission to take one centimetre out of them?'

McKay stood as well, his hands palm up in protest. 'Oh no, not the *Voices for the Animals* thing, Jed. Not you. Grow up, laddie.'

And Jed lunged.

Flynn tackled him before he hit the table.

Du Pont leapt back as McKay stumbled against him.

'I think it's time we left.' Roxie Lockett snatched up the manilla folders in front of her before they could be strewn about the room. 'No point *talking* any more now.' She launched a glare at Flynn, her brother who still had hold of Jed. Then she bent down, eye to eye with Jed. 'See you later.'

Du Pont and McKay brushed themselves off and headed out the door. Roxie followed, kicking the door shut as she left.

Flynn hauled Jed to his feet. 'You nearly did it. You nearly didn't lose your shit.' He gave him a hard shake and let go of Jed's shirt front. 'Congratulations.'

Jed stood for a moment, wiped his hand over his face. 'Yeah. Nearly.' His gaze settled on the lamingtons in the middle of the table. Recalling Du Pont's mouthful of teeth, he said, 'But I think I'm gonna need a bigger cake.'

Two

Rob Carson watched from the edge of the jetty as two men, followed by the gorgeous Roxie Lockett, spilled out of Jed's Boardroom.

That's what the sign said above the door. *Boardroom* with a capital B. Not that big deals, big decisions and big ideas didn't come out of there, but let's face it—*capital* B? It was a shed, for crissakes. Rusty old galv iron, patchy, peeling paint and dodgy timbers holding up the once state-of-the-art 1950s built boat shed. Which was now Jed's HQ for all things Australis Island Dolphin Watch and Marine Adventures.

He ignored the tug on his fishing line. Probably only a passing nudge by a good-sized King George whiting, contempt for the slim bait he'd fixed to the hook and sinker.

Any minute Jed would come stomping out of the ramshackle shed and wave his fist at the clouds. His mop of tangled sun and salt water bleached hair would be stiff on his shoulders. He'd spin back and disappear inside. Rob waited a bit longer, sure that Jed would emerge in full flight and rage against the townies and their idiot notions.

Nope. Jed wasn't about to appear, it seemed.

He waited some more. Maybe Roxie Lockett had calmed him down. Maybe Jed had finally listened to someone. He doubted that as he lifted his line a couple of times to test for any interest in the bait.

Nothing.

Vaguely aware of others near him, he glanced up. Two children, maybe ten-twelve years of age or so were staring at him. He got that a lot. Not that he minded the little kids staring. At least they were honest.

He smiled at them, checked around for their parents. Dad

wasn't far off, ocean gazing, but Mum was also staring at him.

Yep. He got that a lot. He nodded in her direction. 'Afternoon.'

'Afternoon,' she answered after a moment.

Her kids still stared at him. The younger one, the boy, crept alongside. The girl, maybe twelve, gazed moodily then moved off.

'You fishin'?' His dark serious eyes held Rob's gaze. Skinny, nobbly knees and pointy elbows, and feet that looked too small for his thongs.

'Sure am.' Rob bobbed the line again a time or two. 'No bites yet.'

'No bites,' the boy echoed. He sat down by Rob, his gangly legs dangling over the edge of the jetty.

'Be careful, Joshie,' the woman called and came closer to hover a moment. The young girl had wandered off to the bloke still staring off into marine space.

'Mum, I am careful.' The boy looked at Rob. 'What happened to your face?'

'Josh,' the woman admonished.

'Sorry,' the boy mumbled. 'I forgot. I shouldn't ask and all that.' He looked at the water.

''S all right, mate.' Rob glanced at the child's mother, then he turned to the boy. 'Nothing. This is how I came out. Was born like it.' And there was no more surgery he could have to correct the cranio-facial issue. One eye seemed to sit higher in its eye socket than the other, and it bugged out a bit. His cleft palate fix had left his nose misshapen.

'Can I still sit here?' Then Josh remembered something. 'Please?'

''Course you can.'

'I'm sorry. He's very forthright…' Josh's mother at least was open in her approach. 'He truly didn't mean to be rude. He does have manners.'

She didn't seem embarrassed to look at his face, just disconcerted by her son's apparent lapse. Rob's heart warmed a little. *A kid with manners. She woulda taught him that.* She had all the right female curves to fill out her jeans and top. Nice. A plain face; a happy one, it seemed, anyway. Somehow.

He took a sneaky look at the kids' father. *Tall, dark and handsome.* Ah yeah, he would be. The normal-two-parent-two-point-four-children family, the beautiful people.

Shrugging inwardly, he reminded himself that his special derisive voice was only a faint one these days. People had a right to choose their partners from the gene pool. No one wanted a flawed looking human, and that was that. He was so used to believing it, he barely heard himself think it. No point wasting his time on what people thought of how he looked, anyway.

'Do you mind if he sits there? I'm sure he won't disturb the fish.' Long, dark blonde tresses tumbled over her shoulders.

''Course I don't mind. No fish to disturb, I reckon.' Rob lifted his chin, out to sea. 'They're way smarter than me.'

'I'm Josh.'

'Nice to meet you, Josh. I'm Rob.' He loosened a hand from the fishing rod and offered it to the boy who took it in a man's handshake. *Pretty cool.*

'I'm Leonie Miller,' the woman said, and sat on the other side of her son, though she reached across Josh to grip Rob's hand.

Rob nodded. *Very cool.* 'Nice to meet you,' Rob said and briefly returned a smile in the mother's direction. He cast a squint at the husband who still gazed out over the water. The young girl had sidled up to him and was standing snug under his arm.

The line tugged again.

'You got one!' Josh whooped.

'Nah.' Rob bobbed the line up and down. 'I think they're just playing with me today, not taking the bait.'

'Damn,' said Josh.

Rob nodded. 'Damn.'

'Damn,' said Leonie and gave him the biggest gap-toothed grin he'd ever seen.

His heart did a little leap, then he knocked himself mentally on the head. Husband: ten degrees to port, no facial flaws. Self: ugliest human being alive, but with sparkling sense of humour, and a skipper's licence.

No competition, idiot.

'You live here?' Josh asked. A flop of hair came out from behind his ear and he flicked it back, long practised.

'Yep, I do.'

The boy spread his hands. Then, 'Wow. You get to do this all day?'

Rob looked at the dark-haired lad settling in beside him. 'I'm on my day off. I have to work, too, you know.'

Josh nodded. 'Yeah, 'spose. What do you do?'

Rob pointed towards the bay and the moorings off to the north. 'See that boat there, the one with the big writing on it?'

Josh shaded his eyes. '"Australis Island Marine Adventures". Wow, is that yours?'

Rob jiggled his line again. 'Not exactly, but I skipper it.'

'Wow, are you a captain?'

'Sort of.'

'Wow, what sort of boat is it?'

The kid said "wow" a lot.

'It's our *Zeehund*, a rigid inflatable boat. We go out and find pods of dolphins and photograph them to collect information, that sort of stuff.'

'And whales?' The lad's eyes were wide as he stared up at Rob.

'Yep, when they're around. Usually not for a few months yet.'

'Yeah, I know. April to October, right?'

Rob nodded at the boy. 'Yeah. You know your stuff.' He offered a high-five and Josh high-fived back. 'And sometimes even as early as March.'

'Wow.'

'You're making too much noise, Josh,' Leonie said. 'Maybe we better leave Rob to his fishing.'

Rob gave a start when he realised she was smiling at him, and he glanced over his shoulder towards her husband, then back again. He shifted his butt on the jetty timbers.

'Oh,' she said. 'I should introduce my brother, Pete Balfour, and that's Angie with him, my daughter. This is Rob, the skipper of that boat over there.'

Balfour had his shades on his head, not over his eyes. He turned and nodded in Rob's direction. 'G'day. Nice day for it.'

Angie just looked at him, no expression. Well, that was better than some of the looks he got.

Pete Balfour was Leonie's brother. Rob's heart did a little jig thing. She was still beaming at him. He didn't want his heart doing a little jig thing. Nothing but doom down that road.

But Pete was the brother. So where is the husband?

He concentrated on Balfour. Yep, the bro was tall, dark and handsome. In a kinda too-smooth way, almost I'm-too-good-to-be-here kinda way.

'Yeah, nice day, for sure,' Rob agreed.

Balfour nodded again and raised his chin towards the *Zeehund*. 'Australis Island Dolphin Watch, hey?' The young girl detached herself and wandered closer to the wharf edge, took a seat like Josh had done.

The bro. Yep, too smooth, maybe just a little too smarmy. 'Yeah.' Rob juggled his line a bit. Josh, beside him, concentrated on the rod and the line.

Balfour wandered closer, bobbed down on his haunches and peered into the murk. 'You reckon anything'll bite here?'

Rob smelled the subtle aftershave, maybe a whiff of deodorant as well. This guy was pretty together in his RM jeans and his soft leather boots. Way cool. Citified haircut. *Wonder where the Audi is?*

'Plenty to bite, just might not be the day for it.' Rob lifted the rod a little in Balfour's direction. 'You want to sit a while?'

'Nah. Josh can stay awhile.'

'Uncle Pete has to be at a meeting,' Josh said and shuffled closer to Rob and his line. The boy peered into the bait bucket. 'He's in the oil and gas business.'

The air around Rob's face stilled. His fingers tightened on the rod. Even his gut muscles tightened up. Only his eyeballs moved as his gaze bounced from Josh to the boy's uncle. 'Oil and gas business, hey?'

Balfour thrust hands into his pockets. 'Yep. Sorry to bugger up your day. I think your mob and ours are at the meeting table later on.'

Rob nodded. 'I think you're right.' Weird shit. Leonie's brother is The Enemy. Just my freakin' luck.

Leonie piped up. 'Good thing I'm on the dolphin's side.' Her gaze skimmed over Rob then checked out to sea. 'I'm here for a holiday with my kids for a couple of weeks. And, um, we're for dolphins.'

Rob nodded at her, chanced another look at her brother.

Balfour was staring out to sea, again. His brown eyes squinted into the glare and he dropped his sunnies down from on top his head. 'And I'm for jobs,' he said, as if she'd been taking the mickey out of him. He turned and walked away.

Straightening up, Rob handed the rod to Josh. 'Just tug here and there, not often, okay?' He looked over at Leonie and then away again, concentrated on what was left in the bait bucket. Shifted his butt again. 'Thing is, we all know it won't mean local jobs,' he said, keeping his voice low. 'Only locals required will be for the clean-up, and even that'll kill us if the oil spill doesn't.' He heard her silence, loud and clear. Shit. Well, blown it. Still, wouldn't be the first woman who turned her back and walked off for one reason or another.

'I know. Trust me. I've looked into it,' Leonie said. 'We're at loggerheads, my brother and me, but we're on a bit of a holiday, as a family. Except for this one meeting of his.' She caught his eye. 'Pete loves dolphins, really.'

Rob nodded. 'Sure. Trouble is,' he said and rubbed his hands down his pants. 'You can't love 'em on one hand and be in the business of destroying their habitat on the other.'

The woman looked like she was about to speak, but his phone pinged and he grabbed it from his shirt pocket to read the text message.

'Jesus.' He scanned the message again and leapt to his feet. 'Hey, Josh, can you take care of my stuff?' He glanced at the boy and his mother, then at Josh's uncle as he marched away along the boardwalk.

Josh's eyes lit up. 'Oh yeah.'

'Great. I gotta go. Just chuck it back into that shed over there if I'm not back by dark.'

'Oh, wow.'

Leonie frowned. 'What—'

'You want to see how important dolphins are around here? There's a beaching on Red Rocks Bay. We have to get them back in the water, quick, before they dehydrate, or worse.' He loped towards his car parked at the start of the wharf, passed Pete Balfour without a word.

'What could I do there?' she called after him.

But he only waved as he backed up and sped off.

Three

Leonie hadn't wanted to take Angie to the dolphin beaching in case it was too much for her. Leonie herself desperately wanted to go, but who could she leave her daughter with? She had to take her. Pete, after seeing Rob charge past him, had turned back towards them, and Josh was busy with the bloke's fishing rod, engrossed.

'Josh, promise me you'll stay with Uncle Pete,' she said and squeezed his shoulder.

'Yeah.' He didn't see her, she knew that. He was concentrating and pulled the rod and line back as if he was a pro.

He'd be fine; knew enough not to get into the water. And Pete was close.

'Where you going?' her brother yelled as she slipped by him.

'Red Rocks Bay. Look after Josh. Come on, Angie. But you have to be brave.' She and her daughter clambered into the hire car and took off after Rob's four-wheel drive.

By the time she'd found the right road to take her to Red Rocks Bay, and had parked near the water, Rob was metres ahead of them, standing outside at his car with the driver's side door flung wide open. He was trying to climb into wetsuit trunks and hopped barefoot on the sand.

Her daughter jumped out of the car as soon as it stopped. She'd raced to the sand and into the lapping waves. 'Angie, wait,' Leonie shouted,

Angie called over her shoulder. 'Mum, it's okay.'

Startled to hear her daughter's throaty voice, Leonie rushed after her. The low waves pushed against her shins as she watched Angie dart along the shallows towards the first of the beached dolphins. She'd had to wade in a little further than she liked to catch up. 'It's not okay, Angie. Get out of the water so these people can do their jobs.'

The water was calm, thank goodness. Angie stopped. These poor creatures, clearly suffering, stressing, and stuck on the sand on the shore was distressing for her daughter. For her, too.

Leonie looked around as her fingers found Angie's taut little arm. There were eight dolphins, mostly adults from what she could tell, and maybe one youngster not far from where she and her daughter stood.

'But look at them,' Angie cried, her voice raspy, unused. 'They're so close. Why are they so close in this shallow water?'

Her daughter's voice was croaky, as if not practised in speech. It had been a long time since that little voice had sounded, and Leonie nearly burst when she heard it. Shaking herself, not about to make a big song and dance about it right at that minute, she found her own voice.

'We don't know why, sweetheart, but these people here are trying to put them back out into deeper water so we have to let them do that, without getting in the way.' Leonie looked around and saw Rob in the distance with a dozen or so other people. They all moved in what looked like controlled calm from one beached mammal to the other.

Pairs of humans were trying to work out how to encourage a one hundred and sixty kilo dolphin, all soulful eyes and little *squees* to figure it was better back at sea.

Leonie tried to drag Angie back with her, but her twelve-year old was proving her mettle.

'This one's talking to me.' The voice had become stronger, though still with a shake in it, as if the words wouldn't quite come together properly. 'I'm gonna sit with her.' She pointed at the great shape on the sand and took off, knees high in the shallows as she tried to run, pulling her mother.

Him, her. Leonie had no clue. Angie waded across towards her target and Leonie let Angie drag her a metre or two more, then her child sank to her knees in the water alongside a massive mammal.

'Talking to you?' Bigger than she imagined, Leonie stared at the beautiful creature who fixed its sad gaze on her daughter.

A tear popped from its eye as Angie murmured to it.

Leonie dropped beside her daughter. 'We should splash water over him. Her.' Her gaze darted from one group of humans to the other, all desperately working out what to do.

Angie cupped her hands and lifted sea water over her charge, an enormous dolphin whose eye followed her. The girl crooned, sang almost, and Leonie grew breathless as her daughter's tune charged the air around her.

'Come on, Mum, I can't do it quick enough.' Angie had no sooner tossed the husky command over her shoulder before she was back to the crooning.

Leonie lumbered against the sea water rippling to shore. She sat on her heels in the shifting sand on the opposite side of the dolphin. She, too, cupped her hands and imitated her daughter.

Angie's soft voice soon rose to a sort of keening. Still cupping and dumping water, Leonie glanced at Angie only to see rivers of tears pouring down her daughter's face.

'Angie …'

The dolphin's eye on Leonie's side watched her. She cupped water and poured it over the sleek looking skin and began a low hum of her own. She checked in with Angie, their voices blending in a melodious sing-song—was it that old lullaby?

Two men in wet suits clambered over to Angie and Leonie. Over her shoulder, Leonie could see Rob with another four or five others in the shallows. One of whom was a woman with thick, deep auburn curls tied back with a bandanna. Keening quietly, she'd knelt beside another dolphin, and was pouring water from her cupped hands over it. Then she looked up and called to one of the men.

'Jed.'

Mid-stride, Jed turned. Leonie watched as he stared hard at the woman crouched over a distressed animal not much further along. He said, 'Is that—'

'Finluck,' she said, transfixed on him, her tone flat.

Leonie could almost feel the connection between the man and the woman, and the animal on the sand. A primal thing that she understood when she saw tears glistening on the woman's cheeks. *Oh my God, these dolphins are family.*

He took a moment to speak, wiped a hand over his nose and mouth, before he said, 'We'll get this one moving.' He pointed over his shoulder to where Angie sat. 'Ladies, we got this,' he said to Leonie.

He had tucked wiry sun-bleached tangles behind an ear. His lean, hard muscled, salt-dusty legs pushed through the receding tide. Hard to tell his age. Sun browned features crinkled when he spoke. 'We have to get a little moat sort of thing dug around him to keep the water on him, keep him cool before we can get underneath him.'

'It's a she,' Angie cried and laid her hand on the animal's flank.

'Don't touch *her* unnecessarily.' Two other men joined him.

'I'm not.' Angie kept her hand on the dolphin, and her now stout little voice reverted to the gentle croon of her song.

'And keep nice and calm.'

Bewildered, Leonie sat back in the water with her hand hovering over the dolphin and her eye on Angie. Her daughter had spoken very little in nearly six months since the car accident in which Terry, her father, had died. They'd been returning from an access visit when a truck ran a red light and her ex-husband was killed on impact. Angie had been conscious throughout. The medicos said her voice had probably been shocked out of her, that it might take a while before it fully returned as she processed what had happened. And yet here she was, chattering like nothing was wrong, and singing to a dolphin.

The man squatted by her daughter. 'You are doing a great job.

What's your name?'

'Angela.'

'My name's Jed. Angela, we're going to have to move you a little so these guys can get this tarp under him.' He paused. 'Under her, and get her back out to where she belongs.'

Angie still hesitated.

'You know, she might even have a baby out there waiting for us to get his mum back out to sea.'

Angie snatched her hand away and stood quickly.

Leonie staggered to her feet and backed away as the men moved closer around the dolphin whose gaze stayed on Angie. Her heart felt fit to burst when Angie dropped to her knees once more and sang directly to the animal as the men worked.

'Maybe you could keep splashing water on her, too, but be mindful of her blow hole. No water in there, and don't let her blow water get on you, okay?'

Angie nodded and continued crooning. She cupped more water and let it fall on the dolphin's back.

Leonie slid and slipped her way around on the shifting sand to where her daughter sat. She scooped water to ladle over the dolphin's back and sides.

'Nice and easy, keep your voices low and not stressed.' Jed's own voice was a floating rumble on the gentle waves lapping around them. He turned his head to one of the guys. 'Recognise this one, Sammy?'

Sammy shook his head and lifted his camera. He snapped of a few shots before dropping in the sand. 'Not me, not this one. Recorded them all.' He thumbed over his shoulder at other beached dolphins. 'Couple others back there I think we've seen before.' He started to scoop sand away.

Jed pointed to the animal's fin. 'See that, Angela, see those three little nicks in her dorsal fin?' On the top of the fin, near the apex on the trailing edge, three distinct, narrow gouges cut across it. 'That's what we'll use to identify her. Remember that, okay?

We'll call her Three Nicks.'

Angie nodded while Leonie stared. As soon as the other men began dragging out handfuls of sand from around the mammal, their voices dropped to a hum, a rolling, soothing cadence.

Wracking sobs clutched Leonie's throat, and she tried desperately not to sniff. Angie kept singing.

The main man bobbed down beside her. 'Just breathe. She can pick up on your vibe and she'll stress more if she think she's in trouble.' When Leonie glanced up, he beamed at her, a crinkle of tanned skin, zinc cream and a white-toothed grin. 'We need her to know she's in good hands. Don't want her to think we're hopeless bumbling idiots at this.'

Her throat loosened and she swallowed, started singing again.

Angie and Leonie kept the water up as the four men dug a loose trench around the dolphin. One unfolded a long stretcher of heavy-duty canvas, maybe two and a half metres or more which he laid alongside the dolphin. Two poly pipes were pushed through each lengthways edge of it. There were hand holds cut out on either side, and Leonie thought that would be where the men would grip the poles when they needed to lift.

Jed was waving his arm at another small group of men. 'Over here,' he said, lifting his voice a little. Then he turned to Angela. 'Okay, Angela,' he said. 'We're gonna roll her a little this way until we can get her on the sling—' he pointed to the stretcher, 'then we're gonna pull the sling through underneath. Ready, guys?' Nods and grunts acknowledged him. The other men fell in, two on either side. 'You ladies, up you get now and leave us a bit of room.'

Leonie had hold of Angie, who kept crooning, and tugged her out of the way. The dolphin's eye never left her. When they rolled her, Angie moved so she could be seen, her mother in tow.

Once the sling was under, they rolled her again and gently the men positioned the pectoral fins through the gaps in the sling. They were so easy on their charge, so deft and sensitive to the poor animal that Leonie was struck dumb. Tears poured out as she watched the rescue unfold. Her daughter was right there in the midst, crooning and humming quietly.

The men shared each side and slowly, carefully moved the dolphin out to the water. On the sling, the flukes of her tail hung over the end, pointing out to sea.

Leonie waded in after them.

'We have to stabilise her, and lean her a bit more to her side,' Jed said. 'Her internal organs can get shaken around and we don't want any damage done to prevent her getting back out to deep water. Last thing we want is her re-beaching.'

'Oh, God.'

'Dunno that he's got a lot to do with it. But…' He grunted as all eight men lifted the dolphin on top of a wave. 'We have to get her far enough out, turn her around and let her see the way home.' His glance landed on Angie. 'Maybe your daughter can help me out here.'

Angie moved so fast through the water Leonie didn't have time to stop her.

'Okay,' the man said. 'I want you to keep at her eye, right by me. She likes you. Keep singing softly, okay?'

Angie nodded through her crooning. She grabbed hold of Jed's shirt to keep up and a few paces more, they stopped, the water lapping Angie's chest.

'You still got a hold of me, Angela?' Jed asked, looking down at her.

'Yeah.'

'Okay. We're gonna go a bit deeper, so you need to say goodbye now.'

'How—will I keep… How will she know—'

'Just look at her and think it, okay? Like you're talking to her. Just think it.'

Angie concentrated.

Leonie saw her daughter tug reluctantly at the man's shirt but he pulled away with the other men. She let go as he waded further out. He said something, and the men waded strongly, turning as one until the dolphin faced the ocean. Angie tried to follow Jed, stomping through the waves until she could barely stand. Leonie caught up and wrapped her arms around her.

Then, with those few metres gone, the dolphin thrashed its tail and powered off.

Jed turned back in, lifted a hand to hi-five Angie as sea water rolled up and over them. 'You did really well, you're a natural, I reckon.'

One of his mates gave a whoop. 'Look at her *go*.'

Jed turned with Angie and Leonie in time to see their dolphin leap high above the water and shake her body before she re-entered the water.

Angie drew in a sharp breath. 'Was that her? Was that ours?'

'Reckon it was her,' Jed answered. 'Saying 'thanks, and see you later'.'

'Really?' Angie's voice squeaked and her eyes lit up.

Leonie could have cried.

'Yep.' Jed turned and headed in shore. 'Come on,' he said and waved a hand back at her. 'There's more work to do. Another seven of them and about as many of us.'

Angie clambered through the water after him.

Leonie followed along, wading strongly, and clutching Angie's hand. She was glad to feel firmer sand under her feet. 'Jed. Jed?'

'Yep?' Jed powered through the surf back to the beach.

Leonie could see he had his eye on the other rescues. He waved and the red-haired woman on the beach lifted a hand in return. 'How could you tell if it was a female or not?' she asked.

'Tricky unless you turn 'em over. But it wasn't such a big one, so most likely a female.' He powered away from her, pushing into a run in the shallows. He slowed as he came up to the next dolphin.

Leonie stood still in the waves, the sand drawing back under her feet.

Angie pulled her hand free from her mother's and waded ahead on her own. 'It was a female,' she called over her shoulder. Standing still a moment, the small waves buffeted her. 'She told me.'

Four

Pete Balfour sat in the hotel room, his eyes on the laptop screen, earbuds jammed in. The Skype signal hadn't fully loaded. Fingers tapped the desk, feet shuffled, backside shifted side to side on the crappy chair, the vinyl seat cover squelching. If he hadn't known better, he'd swear the thing was winding him up.

Come on, *c'mooon*.

Meeting that bloke on the wharf with the mangled face had rattled him. Not only did he not want to meet any of these fucking dolphin do-gooders, he didn't want any of them to be within cooee of Leonie and the kids.

How to explain to the youngsters that your job puts Flipper in danger? Not that they'd know Flipper. But that every other ocean-going creature was in danger if they got the go ahead for exploration, not to mention the beaches nearby, and the townspeople on the coast whose livelihoods were at stake.

Damn his sister. Damn the kids. His job … He pressed his fingers to his eyes. The headache threatened again.

Reaching across to his satchel, he pulled out the bottle of anti-inflams, the only thing to stop a migraine stone-dead before it got a grip. Three fell into his palm and he downed them with the bottled water he found in the little fridge.

When did he start to have a bloody greenie conscience?

He knew when, all right. The night of his brother-in-law's car accident, and subsequent death. He'd been sort of close to Terry, had maintained a friendship even though his sister's marriage to Terry was going down the gurgler, but his death—so sudden, so fucking final. It changed everything.

Terry had been forty-five. Just starting to live, he'd said. What was that all about? The family was in trouble. Pete talked to him.

Terry had talked about taking the family away, talked about taking holidays, for God's sake, try to patch things up. Get real meaning back between him and Leonie. That he'd lost sight of everything chasing the money.

And just when he'd realised his riches didn't live in the bank account, he woke up dead.

Pete was forty-three. Chased the big bucks, too, chased the women, dodged the altar. Had nothing but money in the bank, in investments, shares. And yet he had nothing to work for … That was wrong. He meant he had no one to work for but himself. No one by his side to work with.

Idiot. Next, you'll be bawling in your porridge.

He rubbed his temples, tried to soothe the pounding at the back of his head. He remembered only a few days ago in his office that he'd nearly handed in his resignation. The boss had blundered in on him. 'I see Ted's got you going down to Australis Island for that meeting with the dolphin rednecks. Take a week or two off, Pete. Grab your sister and take her kids with you.'

Pete had stared at him. 'I am taking a week or two off. The meeting is just a—goodwill gesture.' He wasn't about to tell the boss he'd been scoping out other opportunities for employment so that he could get the hell out of Contour Oil and Gas. *Bloody mob of cowboys.* No wonder the regulator, NOPSEMA—the National Offshore Petroleum Safety and Environmental Management Authority—kept sending them back to the drawing board each time. No surprise there, given their bloody track record.

The boss, a short, wiry, softly spoken man who ruled the department with a rod of iron, shrugged, a lift of a thin shoulder. 'Even a blind man can see you need a break. Terry's death hit all of us.'

Pete had closed his laptop, leaned back in his chair, the draft of his resignation still unfinished. 'He left Leonie and the kids without too much to live on.'

'Yeah. Wake up call, Pete. I don't want to lose you, too. Take some time off after that meeting.' He turned to go, then looked back. 'Get a good result.'

Pete had watched the ramrod straight back disappear down the corridor of cubicles, the snowy-white shock of hair atop the boss's head just visible over the partitions.

Get a good result. Jesus. How could he possibly get a result? He'd read the reports, knew what damage a spill could do in the bight. How could anyone in their right mind say that minimal risk was no risk? Contour Oil and Gas was not the mob to take on the job. It would be a disaster waiting to happen if by some miracle—or madness—NOPSEMA allowed them to drill.

Minimal risk was too much. And every company had risk.

He held his head. Except for a stress migraine every few weeks, he had no real worries about what he did for a living. He just wasn't ready to let go of his job yet, not before he'd secured something else. His job kept him in a shiny new vehicle every couple of years and kept his apartment in the city. And the trips overseas whenever he fancied it ... Or helping his sister.

That was the biggie now. After Terry's death when they discovered that he'd stopped paying his life insurance a year before, Leonie had to sell up the house to keep the kids in school, and to keep up the counselling Angie needed. Her savings hadn't gone much further than Terry's funeral, and whatever investments they'd made as a couple had mysteriously disappeared. The house had to go. At forty-five, Terry's superannuation was the minimum contributed by his employer. There was nothing else.

Pete suspected Terry had been struggling long before the separation, had spent any savings on God-knew-what. So, Pete stepped in after the funeral, and despite Leonie's protests, he'd moved the family into his apartment.

It was no longer the bachelor hang-out it once was. He had kids to look after. Instant fatherhood. Pete could afford it. And he would, for as long as it took. But an apartment was no place for a couple of youngsters to grow up.

So, he had to keep this job. There were no jobs at his level with any greenie mob. And who'd have him anyway? He'd immediately be thought of as some sort of spy; already conspiracies were rife in the industry. There *was* that not-for-profit gig he'd had a look at, the oil spill centre. He reckoned he'd have a lot to offer an organisation like that. Should get in contact.

He rubbed his eyes again, pressed his temples again. At least the throb had eased a bit. He was staring at the screen when Ted Springer's moon face popped up. The man's lips moved. He looked like that gaping fish, the one everyone threw back, even the five-year olds on their first catch.

Then a voice blasted in Pete's ears.

'Hey, Pete, I see you.'

Like he was channelling Shaka bloody Zulu. *Jesus. Flipper. Shaka Zulu. How far back do I go?* Ted's lips had already stopped moving. 'Yeah, Ted. I can see you, too. Wonders of modern technology.'

'What?'

'Never mind. What's the plan? I'm meeting Devereaux and his mobs of clowns this afternoon.'

'Redneck. Just give him the drill. The government's in our pocket, nothing a little outfit like his can do. You're there as a show of good will, camaraderie and all that. Just agree to everything and don't sign anything.'

Pete's eyebrows rose. 'Don't sign anything? Like what? This isn't even an official meeting.'

'Figure of speech.' Ted's face mooned and fish-eyed and danced a panorama around the screen.

Pete blinked to centre his focus. 'The signal's weird, Ted. I'll have to go, I can't hear you clearly and you look—'

'Nod and say yes, smile. They won't know the difference.'

'Yeah right.' Pete deliberately hit the stop button, *delete* and *shut down* as if he'd been interrupted by a signal dropping out.

And Ted Springer was out of his face.

The screen faded to black and Pete waited until it closed altogether. He pressed the lid shut, the final *final* close. Chances are Ted was still talking. That was the scary bit—the man never knew when to shut up, to close a deal, to stitch up a sale. Never knew to just shut-the-fuck-up. Ted would only rile up the locals, instead of cajole. That was Pete's job, which was why he was here and not Ted.

And the useless bastard hadn't given him anything to take to the meeting with Deveraux. Still, as it was only a gesture to the local stake-holders and not official, he'd have to wing it. Why the hell he'd agreed to do it, he couldn't remember right now. It was one thing to try and have a friendly chat with these people, but from Contour's point of view, they were speaking to mentally challenged people. He'd even seen Ted openly roll his eyes at someone's question in one meeting.

Everyone was waiting for a decision from NOPSEMA. It could come down today, or tomorrow. If Contour Oil and Gas didn't get over the line this time, it might mean they'd try again—if they could. Pete didn't believe it. Although they paid well, they weren't the sharpest tools in the oil exploration shed. Then again, if NOPSEMA kept knocking them back, they might decide that drilling in the Great Australian Bight was not financially viable. Always the best excuse to bow out. He hoped they did. *Cowboy mob*.

Shitted off, Pete sat and waited a little while. He'd turn the laptop on again and check for new emails. Might have missed something that would explain why Ted and the company felt it needed to speak to Jed Deveraux and his merry men for the sake of goodwill. Couldn't see it himself. Companies like his ran roughshod over anyone in their way. They had the legal-eagles in their pay, and money to throw at them. A small protest group from the back of Woop-Woop wouldn't be any match for the might his team wielded.

Sure, NOPSEMA would bring down its ruling on the submission, but his company could push the envelope. And they'd site the jobs that oil exploration would bring (he knew hardly any local jobs would be created), what the infrastructure would mean to a place like Australis Island (there'd be almost none, though the spin doctors had it all down pat). They'd make sure the people experiencing a depressed economy would be enraged to think the greenies were holding up jobs, millions in wages, denying the unemployed untold riches by way of new jobs and mega-revenue. Companies like his had always thought they'd win; money talked and all that. But unless they met NOPSEMA's standard requirements, it wasn't gonna happen.

Only the greenies—the real ones, not the political party—mentioned the total devastation of marine life and industry. Interesting how the tourism gurus still hadn't piped up against it. Well, they were all government backed, weren't they?

Yeah, if his company thought it was financially viable, they'd try again. There was a good chance that Contour might not be the viable one.

But this time, Pete wasn't sure he wanted anything to do with drilling for it, exploring for it. If the world had to have petroleum products (how many times had he asked his detractors whether they drove a car or not?), if the world had to have oil rigs somewhere (how many times had he said to someone that their attitude against it just sounded like the NIMBY—*not in my back yard*—bleat), then drilling and exploration had to happen somewhere.

Maybe he should apply to NOPSEMA for a job. Why not? He knew now that he wanted to be part of a group that watch-dogged the winner of the contract—

Or he wanted to be part of an organisation that made sure when an oil spoil occurred that they'd be part of the fix-it process.

The oil spill mob. Australian Waters Oil Spill Response Centre.

Five

Roxie perched on the end of her chair, fingers splayed on the keyboard, and stared at the screen. She couldn't make up her mind whether to laugh, cry or shudder. A mild revulsion had started to bother her since earlier in the day in Jed's boardroom.

Steve McKay's email sat smugly at the top of her inbox. She could always hit delete and pretend never to have received it.

In her hotel room, not far from Jed's shed, she thought back over the aborted meeting earlier and Steve's casual draping of his arm behind her.

He was just a Creep. She always thought of his sleaze-bagginess in capitals. Creep. He had a Belligerent Stare he liked to roll out. Oily Smile was another. Death Breath. Smug Mug. The list went on.

She hadn't taken too much notice of him in the past, even when she'd first started her contract position as Jim du Pont's PA. Steve had weekly meetings in Jim's office. He wasn't only just another work colleague, he topped her as a senior exec. And thankfully had never once tried to have her work for him. Lately though, the intense glances, the quick smiles when there was nothing to smile about, the 'accidental' brushing against her arm, were coming too thick and fast for her to ignore.

Workplace harassment. *Nah*. Sexual harassment, and no calling it otherwise. Pointedly ignoring him hadn't worked. That was the problem—types like him, the more they were ignored, the harder they tried for attention. Like the little shithead boys at school back in the day. They'd pull your hair or smack you to get your attention. Some never grew out of that behaviour.

She pushed back in her chair, ruffled her hair to get some air through it. The thick mass of curls held on to heat like a woollen jumper. Standing, she grabbed the remote and clicked on the air-conditioner. A cool draught of air reached her almost immediately as she sat down again in front of the computer.

The shimmering water of the bay and the strait caught her eye. The midmorning sunlight bounced off the crests of tiny waves further out. Closer to shore the light reflected in the millpond which was the foreshore around the wharf.

Being back on Australis Island felt good. Home was always good. But the reason she was here this time didn't make her feel too good at all. And it was true what she'd said earlier to Jed, about wanting to be in a position to really help.

As usual, Jed hadn't agreed with her. As usual, he thought of it as a betrayal. As usual, the warrior was in full fight mode, and almost without any armour.

Jed. Whatever there'd been between them a long time ago was gone. Sometimes she grew wistful, but mostly she recognised it for what it was—what life should have been, or could have been, or might have been.

The hurt of that had nearly gone.

Jed himself had made it clear they were done, way back seven years ago. They were both twenty-two. He'd gone travelling after he finished his degree and said there were other people they needed to meet in their lives, that they should experience more things. It looked to her that ever since, he had never looked back. Not once. And certainly, not at her.

Yet today she'd noticed the angry flash in his eyes when McKay had touched her.

What was all that about?

No way was she going to tolerate any of Jed's self-righteous explosions of temper, blaming everyone else for it—including her—and let him think he was going to get away with it. He wouldn't get by dealing with people by yelling at them or leaping over tables to grapple people by their shirt-fronts. Even if it was Steve McKay.

Jeez, leaping across the table like that, he could've squashed Berta's lamingtons. Then there'd really have been hell to pay. A little smile wouldn't be denied, and then she burst out laughing. She wished she could have seen McKay's face, but all she saw was Jed's lunge, and Flynn, her brother, grab at him. Lamingtons saved. She knew the two boys would have breathed a sigh of relief about that. No one wanted an enraged Berta.

The email drew her attention again. Though its content seemed harmless enough, McKay was only a few doors down in another room in the same hotel. If she answered him, he'd be along the corridor quicker than a poison dart.

Her lip curled now. She'd have to nip it in the bud—or at least, chop it right off before it went full blown. Another laugh at the analogy, and then a sobering thought.

A rebuff might cost her a job.

Her fingers settled on the keyboard again, waiting for the command to send a reply.

She snatched them away. *No, dammit. He can wait.* She wasn't on the job now, and the meeting with the oil and gas guy wasn't until four o'clock.

She'd email a reply to Steve at three forty-five, and deal with him face-to-face after the meeting. Happy with that, she jumped a mile when her phone pinged an incoming text. *Oh no—the lech is gonna push it by texting.*

Instead, it was Jed messaging.

Pod of 9 bchd RR Bay. Need u

Fingers shaking, she answered. **Be 15**

Her wetsuit was in her vehicle. Slipping boaties on her bare feet, she grabbed her handbag, her sunnies and a hat, bolted out of her room, and down the stairs.

Nine beasties. Would be a super big job even if they had enough people. There'd be the constant juggle as to which department needed to take control, which *experts* had *the* expert advice, which volunteers could and couldn't help, which—

Bugger it.

She ran to her car and climbed in.

We need to get them out to deep water. God only knows what time we'll be back. She'd text Jim that she'd be late for the meeting. He'd have to let the oil and gas guy know.

Six

Pete Balfour checked his watch again. Four fifteen. *Where the bloody hell is everyone?*

He strode back to the hotel's front counter and spoke to the receptionist. 'Sorry to bug you again, but you're sure the meeting with Dolphin Watch is in that room there?' He thumbed over his shoulder at the cavernous conference suite he'd just left.

'Absolutely sure,' the man said. He checked a list in front of him and ran his finger down the lines. His badge said his name was Todd Evans, Day Manager. 'There it is, right there. Meeting Room Three.'

Pete leaned over a little and checked as well. Yep. 'And the time?'

'Booked for four pm today.' Todd looked up, expecting another question. When none was forthcoming, he volunteered, 'We heard there was a pod of nine dolphins beached at Red Rocks Bay. The Watch team would go and assist, I'm sure. Maybe that's why they're late.'

'Great.' Pete turned to go, then back again. 'Thanks. I'll wait just a bit longer.'

He pulled his phone from his coat pocket, keyed in Leonie's number. He'd let her know that the meeting was probably not going to happen and that he'd come and get them to go for an early pizza dinner. Bemused when message-bank picked up, he clipped out a short few words asking her to text him her whereabouts. He closed off and continued to pace.

Returning to the conference room, he headed toward the windows. He stood in front of uninterrupted views of the sheltered bay, and beyond that, was the headland at the eastern end of the island. Sixty k's drive by road, he knew, maybe ten k's as the crows flies across the bay and the inlet to the other side. A light haze sat on the shoreline beyond.

The calm water in front of him at the hotel's little beach was almost without a ripple. It reflected a few clouds that studded a bright and pale blue sky, and without even a hint of breeze, there was barely a drift in them. A pair of pelicans glided overhead like graceful, enormous sentinels. He watched until they disappeared far off to the right of the hotel and the little bluff beyond.

Standing stock still, in silence, and with an unusual quiet all around him, he became aware of a series of vehicles pulling up into car parks below.

Out spilled Angie and Leonie from her car. Then two other men, wearing only board-shorts and zinc-cream, piled out from the back seat, clutching wetsuits.

Pete focused. *Who—*

Then a big four-wheel drive emptied another five men, all in the same beach uniform, mostly either wetsuit shorts or boardies. One of them was Jed Deveraux. He recognised the tall man and his mess of sun-bleached matted hair from the photos Contour had supplied.

Deveraux's face split in a big grin and he waved across at someone. When Pete glanced, he saw Leonie wave back. An excited Angie jumped up and down and she waved as well.

Angie? *Angie* was waving at someone and smiling and laughing?

Then, a third vehicle pulled up and demobbed its passengers. Three blokes, again in assorted beach duds and neon war-paint spread across noses and cheeks and ears.

The last to exit was the driver, a woman. And what an exit. Built, and tall, she had masses of deep auburn twists loosely tied at the back of her head. Her wetsuit was half mast, the shoulders and arms dangling at her waist, her hips and legs still encased. The top she wore was still damp in places, and as she bent to retrieve something out of her car, it gaped to reveal a glimpse of tanned breasts encased in a smooth bra. She bobbed back, leaned on the roof of the vehicle, and called out.

Deveraux turned and shouted back to her, waved his hand towards where Pete was standing. Then everyone turned to look up at him. *Caught me gawking like a bloody school kid, dammit.*

The woman's gaze met Pete's for a moment. He stared back. She ducked into the car and grabbed out a bag, maybe her handbag, but the thing was big enough to put a small car into. Her glance flicked up once again, then she reefed about in the bag and pulled out her mobile phone.

Someone waving their arms caught his eye. Leonie. She cupped her hands against her mouth and mimed something.

Pete shrugged, spread his hands. *What?*

Then Leonie pulled a face at him and levelled a hand at chest high.

What? Jeez—Josh. Shit shit shit. The wharf—how long had the little tacker been sitting on the wharf? *Shit.* He'd left him there with that bloke's fishing gear. Forgotten him. *Shit!*

He slapped his forehead and instantly Leonie knew what he meant. She spun around, pulled Angie with her and ran along the walkway leading to the jetty.

Shit shit shit

Paralysed for an instant, he stared at her then saw that Rob guy slide his vehicle into a vacant car park. Rob hung out the window, waved his arms at Jed who shrugged, said something and pointed. Rob then backed up and floored his vehicle in the direction of the wharf.

Pete bolted out of the conference room, through the lobby, down the steps to the pavement and sprinted across the road. All he could hope was that Josh was still where he'd left him, sitting on the wharf with the fishing rod.

He pounded down the road, scanning the wharf for any sign of his nephew. *Please be there, please be there ...*

Either way he was dead meat. His sister would kill him six ways to Sunday.

Seven

Evie curled a finger under a slip of hair clinging to her face and tucked it back behind her ear. She looked over Josh's head. 'I think you're right. Looks like the whole tribe is galloping towards you. Good thing you stayed here.'

Josh looked to his right. 'Yeah. That's mum, and my sister Angie in front, waving their arms an' yelling. Then there's that Rob guy I met before, and Uncle Pete behind him. Gee, they're runnin' fast. Somethin' musta happened.' He tugged the fishing line and reeled it in. 'But they're gonna be so happy I've caught all these fish.'

'Yep, they sure will.' Evie craned her neck and spotted the others milling in the carpark. Jed towered above most of them and she smiled to herself. He stretched his arms high over his head, then hauled himself up to stand on the roof of his car. He waved in her direction and she waved back.

The woman Josh had pointed out as his mum, yelled from about twenty metres away. 'Josh!'

Josh waved his hand impatiently. 'Stop yelling,' he called. 'You'll scare all the fish.'

Evie jumped to her feet. 'Hi. I'm Evie Prior.'

'Leonie Miller.' She looked out of breath, anxious, bewildered and angry all at once. 'What on earth …'

Evie shrugged. 'I work with Rob and the Dolphin Watch team.' Shoving her hands in her cargo pants pockets, she said, 'Josh told me you'd all gone off somewhere, and that he had Rob's rod and lines to look after. So, I figured he might need the company till you all came back.'

Leonie exhaled loudly, a relieved sob escaped. 'Thank you.'

Rob skidded to a halt beside Josh. 'You all right, kid?'

'I got eight.' Josh lifted his chin towards the bucket, adjusted the hat he wore. 'Finished up all the bait.'

'Did you get fish, Joshie?' Angie hunkered down and sat herself on the jetty beside her brother.

'Yep.' He gave her a long, odd stare, then ducked to look around his mother to see a man slow up alongside, also out of breath. 'Hi, Uncle Pete.'

'Hi, Josh.'

Evie looked from one to the other. Rob had settled himself down on the boy's other side. Leonie and this Uncle Pete only glared at each other.

'I'm sorry,' Uncle Pete said to the boy's mother, his hands spread. 'I just—'

'Forgot.' Leonie rubbed her nose. 'You just plain forgot.'

'Forgot,' he agreed, and ducked his head. 'Sorry.' He too shoved his hands in his pockets and turned away. 'Josh. Sorry, mate. I forgot you were sitting here.'

'It's cool. I was okay.'

Uncle Pete nodded. Evie almost felt sorry for him. 'Well, I can get going, now,' she said and slipped between Leonie and Uncle Pete and stopped behind Rob. 'We taking *Zeehund* out, Rob? We needed at Red Rocks Bay?'

'No.' Rob was peering into his bucket and reached in to pull out a thirty-centimetre King George whiting. He made a face of approval and put it back. 'Parks and Wildlife reckon they got it under control. Maybe tomorrow to make sure none of them blundered their way back.'

Josh spun around to face Rob. 'Can I come, too?' His face lit up.

Rob twisted to see Leonie had shaken her head but had let her brother off the hook. 'Wanna come out in the boat tomorrow?' he asked her. 'You and the kids?'

'Mum?' Angie's eyes had widened.

'Mum!' Josh demanded an answer.

Leonie held her hands up to the kids. 'All right. If Rob thinks it's okay.'

Evie saw the smile split Rob's features. *Now, that isn't something you see every day.* She glanced at Leonie who was grinning right back at him.

'Sure, it's okay. Let me have your phone number.' Rob felt in his tackle box and brought out his phone. 'I'll call you with a time, what to bring, what to wear.'

Leonie rattled off her number and Rob keyed it into his contacts.

Evie blinked and turned away, hiding a smile. *Well, will you look at that?* 'I'll see you all later, then,' she called over her shoulder. As she wandered off, she had Jed in her sights, and headed for the carpark

Now that he was back, she wondered if the meeting was going to go ahead with the oil and gas guy. They were way late, hardly dressed right, probably pumped getting the beasties back out to deep water. Probably knackered, as well.

Still, Jed didn't look knackered. He sat on the roof of his car until she came closer, then slid to the ground, a big smile on his sun-browned face. The smear of white zinc cream across his nose and cheeks had sand in it. 'Hi, Evie. Missed a good beaching.'

She pulled a face. There was never a good beaching. 'How many did we win back?'

'All but an oldie.' He reached out a hand and she grabbed it. 'Probably too tired. He just didn't seem to want to stay out. The others took him out after we floated him, but he came right back. We had to let him.' He blew out a long breath. 'He might have been the reason the others came in, trying to look after him. Anyhow, Parks have taken over, and they'll do a necropsy.'

Evie screwed up her nose. 'You know, no matter how long I've been doing this, I'll never get used to autopsies for animals being called that,' she said. 'Sounds creepy.'

Jed looked bemused. 'Does it?'

Flynn Lockett wandered around, a towel draped over his broad shoulders, his wetsuit open and shucked to his waist. 'It was team work, Evie. No fights.' He grinned at her. 'Not even a yell out of the golden-haired boy here.' He rubbed the towel over dark auburn chest hair.

'Yeah, I'm stepping up,' Jed said. 'All under control.'

Evie tapped her fist to his shoulder. 'Good for you.' Then she noticed Flynn's sister, Roxie heading towards them. *Great*. She was Jed's bloody prickly ex-girlfriend from yonks ago.

Roxie had her wetsuit off to the waist, too. She was pulling on a windcheater over her tank top, her mop of hair caught up in a thick scrunchie. 'I'm guessing the meeting's been called off. Probably not a bad thing.' Then, all polite and everything, said, 'Hi, Evie.'

'Hi, Roxie.' Evie wasn't going to let old politics get in her way; Jed and Roxie were done and dusted long before she ever came on the scene, so Jed had said. She sucked in a breath. 'I haven't heard anything about the meeting being called off. Anyone know?'

Jed shook his head. 'Let's just pile up to the hotel and see if someone's still there.'

'I'll make grovelling apologies if necessary,' Evie said. 'A PA's job, no doubt.'

'We don't need brownie points,' Jed said. 'If they give a toss, being at Red Rocks Bay trumps any meeting with them. We'll just reschedule. It's not like it's the real deal. The guy's just on his own time.' He looked over Evie's head to where she'd just come from. 'Who's Rob bringing back with him?'

Evie followed Jed's gaze. Rob was heading towards them, rod, line and bucket in his hands, the woman on one side of him and the boy on the other. A man and a young girl brought up the rear. 'A visiting family. The kids belong to the woman, and the bloke is the kids' uncle.'

'Talent for the survey trip tomorrow?'

'Yeah. Rob's already asked them to come on board.'

'That bloke might want to get out of those fancy duds.' Jed was staring at the man holding the young girl's hand.

Roxie squinted at the group as they came closer, recognising him. 'He was in the conference room as we pulled up in the carpark.'

'That bloke?' Jed tilted his head again at the approaching group.

Roxie frowned some more. 'Yeah. Maybe he's the oil and gas guy.'

'In that case,' Jed said. 'Reckon we could still crank up this meeting after all.' He reached across and grabbed Flynn's towel, threw it over his shoulders and tugged it back and forth, drying off. 'There. Now I'm dressed for it.' He flung the towel back at Flynn. 'Let's go.'

Roxie called out. 'He might not be the guy, though.'

'You find out,' Jed threw over his shoulder. 'Meet you in the bar.' He strode off.

'Put a shirt on.' Evie was talking to his back. She looked at Roxie. 'I'll be the only one with money for drinks. See you up there.' She smiled as she went ahead, felt a little smug when Roxie looked at her with an odd expression. She followed Jed up the path.

Eight

Roxie stood by. The man in the suit pants and with the hangdog look on his face glanced at her, once, maybe twice. Then when he was level with her, he smiled, right at her. Right into her eyes. He still had hold of the little girl's hand. He moved on.

The family and Rob dawdled past her.

'Hey, Rox,' Rob greeted, and flicked her shoulder with a finger as he passed. He bent closer to the boy to hear what was being said to him.

'Hey, Rob,' she answered and hoped she didn't look distracted. Not that he noticed. The woman beside him wasn't taking any notice of Roxie either, had barely flicked her a glance, or a quick smile. Her eyes were on Rob.

How do you like that?

Roxie brought her attention back to the man and little girl. She bet that this bloke—this dark-haired guy with the interested gaze in his eyes—was the oil and gas guy, and there he was, only a moment ago, flirting with her. Wouldn't he get a big surprise in about twenty minutes.

High overhead, cloud cover had crept over what had been a bright blue sky. The afternoon heat thrummed through it, the humidity dense. The wetsuit was suffocating, so she made a bee-line back to her car and grabbed the clothes she'd worn before arriving at Red Rocks. Tucking them under her arm, she fled across the street and up to her hotel room.

No time for a quick shower. The others were all at the pub and if nothing else, her presence might soothe any feathers about to be ruffled.

She hopped and stomped about the suite trying to tug off the wetsuit and fell on the bed to wrench off the last of it. Always tough going on your own.

Pulling on cargo pants, and shrugging on a cotton shirt, she grappled her hair into a coil and shoved in a large tortoise-shell hair-clip. It wouldn't hold, she knew, but it was better than straggly wet coils of salt-crusted hair looking daggy on her shoulders. Feet in boaties again, she grabbed her bag and lunged out the door.

And bumped smack-bang into Steve McKay.

'Couldn't have done it better if I'd practised it,' he said, and steadied her with a grip on her arm.

She had to pull herself free. 'Sorry. Gotta run.'

'Where to?' He held up his hands but stood in her way.

No point avoiding it. 'Pub. The meeting with the oil and gas guy.' She dodged around him but he followed.

'Might come along. Was heading for the pub anyway.' Oily Smile.

Roxie tried not to curl her lip as she dashed to the stairs and raced down, not waiting. She hoped he'd get the message that she was *so* not interested.

Last thing she heard before she hit the ground floor was his footfalls on the landing above. 'Maybe we'll catch up for a drink after.' At least his voice was drifting far behind her.

She didn't answer. *Not if I can help it.*

Shoving open the heavy glass doors, she spotted Jed leaning over a table laden with so many papers and folders and books it looked like her office at work.

The oil and gas guy—what the hell was his name? He was stabbing a finger over a map, insisting Jed take notice.

Jed. Tall, with sun bleached blondy-browny tightly curled hair that bobbed on his tanned shoulders in man-ringlets, still had a zinc-creamed face. A well-muscled partly clothed body. His gaze fierce, he peered down, silent. *If only, if only. But no way now.*

Oil and gas guy. Tall, dark hair, wavy and shiny clean, frowning, broad strong hands expressive, determined, fully clothed, animated. *Just plain no way.*

Roxie stopped near the bar and rested her hand on it, steadying. She knew she should get closer—damn, how she hated 'should'—but it wasn't looking pleasant. She'd seen Jed in these discussions before, knew what it looked like and right now it looked like his boiler was about to burst.

Where was Flynn? Glancing about, she found her brother lounging on the far wall, and his intense gaze was on the other two men. Flynn was no doubt watching, but if Jed blew, nothing would stop it.

She made her way over to her brother. 'So far?' she asked and lifted her chin in Jed's direction.

'He's barely holding it in. I reckon we need to stop that other guy banging on so much and get seated at the table.' Flynn pushed off the wall, his arms still folded. 'Look, I don't need this little get together to go overboard and have to clean up a bloody mess. I've got enough on my plate wading through the timber mob's Environmental Impact Statement. Seen Evie?'

Roxie shook her head. 'Not this minute. Thought she—'

Evie flung into the room, arms full of bedraggled paperwork. Jed looked up at her.

'Here we go,' Flynn muttered and uncoiled. 'I should get her to give me a hand with the EIS before she stirs Jed up.'

Roxie glanced from her brother, to Jed to Evie. Jed's intense stare was on his PA, and vice versa. 'Stir him up? I thought she was supposed to have a calming effect.'

'Yeah, right,' Flynn said, then called out, 'Let's all get down to it over here.' He stabbed a finger at two tables, joined horizontally. 'That way,' he muttered. 'They can eyeball each other. Too far to launch full bodied across the table. Then I can get on with my job.'

Jed and Evie moved to one table, the O&G guy to the other. Steve wandered in, a beer in his hands. Roxie groaned inwardly. Wherever she sat, there'd be a spare seat beside her.

Jed looked at McKay. 'Where's your off-sider, Steve? Still talking to Canberra?'

Steve smirked around him, flicked a glance over Roxie. 'No idea. I'm just here to have a drink with Roxie, and to check the entertainment.'

Eye roll. Roxie plopped into a seat opposite the O&G guy who looked up.

'Pete Balfour,' he said and stood, outstretching his hand across the table.

Roxie leaned over and took the broad hand, its grip warm but not crushing, not lingering. Professional. He only made minimal eye contact. 'Roxie Lockett.' She sat back. Tasted salt on her lips and hoped she didn't look like some old boatie off the wharf.

Jed flicked her a glance, narrowing his gaze. *And you can go to hell, Jed Deveraux.* Roxie noticed Evie sidled closer to him. *Good on you, Evie. Staking your claim. You poor kid.*

'Do we have a facilitator?' Steve asked, nursing his beer as he took a seat alongside Roxie. 'Someone to keep tempers cool and the discussion on track.'

Pete Balfour's eyes glanced between her and McKay. Roxie inched away from the older man, enough to be noticeable, but she didn't make eye contact with anyone to check. *They'll be beating chests, next.*

'My temper's cool.' Jed lifted his eyebrows and gazed around.

'Won't be for long,' Steve said and swigged from the beer.

Evie grabbed Jed's wrist and squeezed. Flynn sat opposite Jed eyeballing him.

Oh yeah, Roxie thought, watching. *Just a matter of time. How many enemies we got here?* Glancing up, her gaze collided with Balfour's. He was one.

He didn't bat an eyelid for a moment or two then flicked his glance down to the papers he had open in front of him. 'Let's get underway. And why do we have need of a facilitator?' He poked about in his shirt pocket, withdrew wire-rimmed reading glasses and slipped them on. He looked over at everyone. 'This is just a chat.'

'You might have to rethink that,' Steve again, smug, eyeballing Jed.

Jed leaned forward, pointing at him. 'What are you even doing here? Why don't you just get the f—'

'No, we don't have a facilitator.' Evie shot to her feet. 'We should be able to get through this without a punch-up or chest-thumping.' She glared at Jed till he looked away. 'It's just a friendly meeting, nothing formal, right?'

Go girl. Roxie's estimation of Evie rose a little. 'Yeah, Steve. Shut up,' Roxie said sideways. 'This isn't your gig.'

She heard him sniff, swallow another chug of beer. There goes her job, the moment he gets back to tattle to Jim du Pont, she thought, and sighed inwardly. But that didn't feel as bad as she first thought it would. Maybe if she came back to the island Flynn would let her stay in the old settler's cottage on his block. *Shit.* One spoilt-brat sniff from Steve McKay and now she was thinking of moving back home. *What is this?* But why not? She was hardly happy in the job at the university. Certainly not happy working with Lecher-Guts Steve McKay. And really, what good was she doing over there? *Time to rethink, Roxie, old girl.* The thought made her sweat, but despite that, excitement trilled in her stomach.

The oil and gas guy took her attention again. 'Thanks, everyone, for coming along today,' he said. 'I'm Pete Balfour. I guess you know I'm from Contour Oil and Gas and that we're behind the push to explore for oil in your region.' He lifted his head to eyeball Jed. 'We all expect to hear from NOPSEMA in the next few days.'

'So what do you want here with us?' Jed asked. 'It's a no-brainer. You'll get knocked out.'

Balfour gave him a glance but didn't take the bait. 'I know others before me have barged in, been ignorant toward people who have grievances about things.'

'The grievances are real, backed up by science.'

'And that in the past you feel like you're not being heard by us.

We do hear, we do listen. We've got safeguards in place.'

'Bullshit. Nothing's safeguarded by the look of your submission except the massive dollars you'll take out of the ocean while destroying it and everything in it. Then you'll run, leaving us with the fuckin' mess.'

Flynn leaned forward. 'Jed.'

'And we know there's very minimal risk of a spill,' Balfour finished, without even acknowledging anyone had interrupted.

'That's too much risk.' Jed bunched his fists on the table. 'And it's not just the spill once the thing is in situ. It's the exploration before that happens. The boom of the seismic airguns deafens cetaceans—that's *all* aquatic mammals.'

'We know you're fully aware of the issues we addressed,' Balfour went on.

'Being deaf means that they can't communicate,' Jed ground out. He tapped the table. 'They can't find mates, or food because they can't hear, which is the sense they rely on. It's their major sensor, like we rely on our sight.'

Balfour looked at Jed, kept his features stony. He said, 'Companies like ours have the science on board. We need the marine biologists, to assist, and we have them.'

Jed snorted. 'I live here. I work here. It's a pristine area. I can't be a marine biologist, and not be a conservationist. You've only put the token expert on board to make it look like you've got it right. But it doesn't work like that.'

The O&G guy went on, taking a deep breath, keeping his voice even. 'Best practice oil and gas companies—with the money—will meet whatever requirements NOPSEMA hands down. What you want is at least a responsible operator in the area.'

'We don't want any one of them in the area.'

'Well, you've got them, mate,' Balfour said, directly at Jed. 'They're coming, and no amount of protest will stop them. If it's financially viable, and they meet the NOPSEMA requirements they will drill in the bight. Best thing to do is hold them to account.'

'After the fuckin' spill event?' Jed yelled.

And from there it all went downhill fast.

Nine

Pete Balfour gathered up his papers that had landed on the floor after Devereaux upended the table. He shuffled them between satchel and folder. Well aware that Roxie Lockett lingered, maybe to talk, he kept his head down. He didn't like it. She was no pushover. Finally, all paperwork was back in its order. He had no excuse not to look up.

'That went well,' she said. She leaned on the edge of a table and folded her arms.

He lifted a shoulder. 'I'm used to it. Tempers heat up, voices get louder, guys swear, get punchy.' He parked his backside on a table facing her. 'Up end tables.'

'Where does it get you?'

Her gaze, intense, her voice soft yet terse, hit him in the chest and something furrowed deep, like an arrow releasing pressure. Heat poured out and he felt his face burn. 'Get me? It gets my message over. We are going to test. We are going to drill. We are going to sink deep bores. We are going to be in the neighbourhood. If we get the approval, we'll go ahead. Simple as that.'

'And we'll do our best to stop you. She cocked her head and some of the damp, tight coils of her hair drifted out of the clip thing and fell onto her shoulders. 'We know that the noise from the drilling, and the use of a vertical seismic profile catastrophically impacts—'

He held up a hand. 'Save the sermon. I know all about VSP. Heard it all before. A smart woman like you would know how it works.' Roxie sucked in her cheeks but he ignored it. 'Near-field and far-field received sound levels are influenced by lots of factors.'

'That all sounds like weasel words to me. We know all too well what's going on with VSP.' Her gaze nailed him. 'And you don't care about the impact. Don't you believe what it does to all those animals nearby?'

There she had him. He knew its effects. He dropped his chin to his chest. 'Nothing to do with what I believe.'

'You are joking,' Roxie said. 'It has everything to do with what you believe.'

He looked out to sea. She nailed him, all right. She was so intent watching for his response that she didn't miss a thing, and he knew it. 'I have a job to do. Today I addressed this meeting of—' he waved his hand at the last of the people leaving the room, 'Locals, on my own time, I might add. It was a request from my boss just because I was taking a few days off here, to put forward the exploration proposal in layman's terms, just a chat, nothing formal.'

'Layman's terms? We're not idiots here.'

'I didn't say that.'

'By the sounds of it, maybe your mob hung you out to dry.'

Pete had wondered that himself. How much of a stooge was he—or how stupid—agreeing to do it alone, without the team?

Roxie straightened up. 'Put forward the proposal to what outcome?'

This was the part where Pete felt even more uncomfortable. He knew it wouldn't matter what the outcome of the meeting was, it wouldn't change a thing. 'To gauge community reception. Resistance.'

'You already know that. We don't want you here. No drilling. Simple.'

He shrugged. 'There'll be jobs. And there are people here on the island who want to see us go ahead.'

Roxie snorted. 'The mayor, you mean?'

'And others.'

'For heaven's sake,' Roxie said, exasperated. 'She's just making noise because she can. Thinks it keeps happy ratepayers, people on her side for the next council election. She forgets she needs to keep a younger, savvy generation on side, needs to keep their livelihoods sustainable. But it's not a council issue. She's got no say in any of this, she's just got a loud—' She scratched her head and looked at him. 'Voice.'

'If she's on our side, she's a voice for exploration, for jobs.'

'Only because it doesn't impact her patch immediately. Ask her about the proposed deep-sea port in pristine Jones Bay right near her place, and all those jobs they reckon they'll have. She's been yelling blue-bloody-murder about that. Reckons it'll degrade land prices. Won't be the half of it if our coast is hit with an oil spill.'

Pete drew in a deep breath. 'Jones Bay is not my patch. Look, I've got a job and it's important to me. There are not many job opportunities for people on the island so why wouldn't creating jobs be important around here?'

'Oil exploration won't create jobs. Thing is,' Roxie said. 'The people who want to work, already work. Maybe not at exactly what they want, but there's work. Unless you're offering the kids who live here apprenticeships in trades or traineeships, or a chance for uni via scholarships for degrees in engineering or something, how are you going to create jobs?'

'I went through all that at the meeting.'

'These kids will still need qualifications. And the FIFO gig—fly in and fly out of here? Hardly creating jobs for locals.'

'Some locals might have that opportunity. Most FIFOs will come if there's advantage. They'll need their morning coffee at the deli, or their local pizza when they're here. They'll use the local shops.'

'You know as well as I do that a rig in the bight won't create local jobs.'

'It will.' He looked at her, his gaze stubborn.

Roxie shifted away from the table and walked to her bag. 'You haven't convinced me, or any of us, I reckon.' She grabbed papers from a nearby desk and stuffed them into it. 'We need jobs here that will sustain our lifestyle.'

'Good luck with that, no matter what you do, or where you are.'

'We need to give our youngsters something to work towards.'

'You need industry here and you don't have any. The kids here need to be willing to work.' He heard his voice rising. 'You need to manufacture stuff, export stuff, and all you all do is resist the businesses that want to do that. You need to be open all year round.'

She looked at him. 'And we've heard all that before. There's no magic wand for here, no flick of a switch. But what we don't need is a cowboy outfit coming to our ocean and decimating our marine life, our beaches, our aquaculture, taking the money and running. And that's without the oil spill.'

Pete squinted. *Oil spill.* It was everything Contour Oil and Gas tried to downplay wherever they went, citing minimal risk. 'There might not even *be* an oil spill. The number of spills compared to the number of rigs—'

'It's not only the spill. It's the actual exploration for oil. And if you get the licence to drill, there will be an oil spill.'

He waved that off. 'The spill response these days in Australia is the world's best.'

She wasn't letting up. 'Nothing survives an oil spill. Once it's spilled, it's never not there. Even the so-called clean-up is as bad as the spill itself.'

'Not any more, it's not. Oil spill response is doing some good work. You won't hear much about it. They like to keep their organisation under wraps, out of the spotlight, keep things independent.' He wasn't about to say he was looking for a job with them—he'd keep that under his hat.

'Independent? Oh come on—you guys are members of their organisation. That's public knowledge. How is that independent?'

Only bloody public knowledge if you go looking for it. 'It is independent. One hundred per cent.' He could feel the prickles on the back of his neck. She was gonna be a pain in the arse.

'You oil and gas guys would've done your homework on the clean-up detergent. So have we, and what we found says it's a bit different to what you're saying it is.' She shoved her hands in her pockets. 'Despite mobs like yours telling us not to believe the "silly science on the internet", that *Corexit 9500*—as an example—is a reagent, and no amount of calling it a surfactant is going to change the toxicity of it.' She shook her head. 'As harmless as kitchen sink detergents, we're told. I don't think. Perhaps that oil spill response centre of yours needs to brush up on their understanding of the reports in the scientific journals.'

Heat fired up his back and across his chest. *Keep the lid on. Keep the lid on.* She'd just given it to him both barrels. She'd known about the spill response mob, about their work. He'd revisit the website, get up to speed. Use better arguments. *Dammit*—he should've have been all over it. He'd got slack, thought this Australis Island pack was a bunch of rednecks—he should have known better, known not to take Ted at his word.

'And then there's the question of the stacking cap,' she said, her fierce gaze on him. 'Closest one is thirty-five days from the bight. *Days*. You need one on site—that's one of our demands, something what we want you to ensure is on all your rigs. Proactive co-operation to do the right thing, not reactive blame and shame. It's too late then.'

'Won't happen.' His jaw clenched, otherwise, jeez, he was going to erupt like Jed Devereaux. Drilling in the bight was about bloody corporation and government mega-bucks, not about the welfare of some whiny greenie mob on a hick island in the Southern Ocean, nor about some coupla hundred whales and dolphins. He pushed off the table and gathered his paperwork. 'So, it appears there's nothing to talk about. Our opinions are poles apart.' He zipped his bag shut. 'I get it. See you later.' He walked off. He knew it was childish. He knew that as long as he had his job with Contour Oil and Gas, the only argument he had was the same old argument.

Jesus. He'd submit his resumé to the spill centre regardless of an opening. Now is the right time. He'd hound them for a job, get out of Contour.

The calculating look on Roxie's face needled him. Even if he did feel like shit, he still needed a big paying job. An exec's pay, one hundred and eighty k per annum, went a long way to housing, feeding and educating his sister's kids. Not far enough, but for the moment he couldn't slip up on that. He should have realised how lucky he was before Terry had the accident. He would have put more of that salary away, been smarter with his money. *Oh come on.* How was he to know he'd step up and keep his sister—where had that come from?

*

It didn't take anywhere near as long as Roxie thought it would. Steve McKay was in the bar waiting for her as she came out after Pete Balfour. But Steve wouldn't have had time to get to Jim du Pont yet, so what was he up to?

She groaned inwardly. She knew.

'Have a drink, Roxie?' He wasn't smiling the Oily Smile this time.

'No thanks. I'm going back to my room to do some work.'

He pushed off the bar and stepped in front of her. 'Before you go, I just wanna say that you don't get to tell me to shut up in public. Or anywhere, as a matter of fact, especially in meetings. I'm gonna write you up a first warning.'

That stopped her cold. Not because her job would be on the line but because the first warning of three could sometimes be more of a bullying threat than most people realised. It put you on notice that your every move would be watched, specifically at times to have you trip up on the slightest transgression, earning yourself a second warning. Not many smart people stayed around for the third and final. Too bloody humiliating going through the process.

And if you were lucky enough to win a wrongful dismissal, good luck finding another decent job.

This coming, she admitted to herself, had been only a matter of time. Suddenly, she was over it. Another nod from the universe. 'Go your hardest, Steve.'

He went to grab her arm and thought better of it. 'You'll regret it.' He added a Belligerent Stare.

Laughable. How many beers had he had already? She threw her hands up, warding him off. She didn't want him in her sight and backed off, closing any more conversation. No way did she want him hassling her. 'Just keep your distance.'

'You all right?'

She spun around. Pete Balfour had come back to the bar. His gaze was on her, not on Steve McKay, who'd made his way out of the hotel corridor in a hurry.

'I'm good. Thought you'd bolted.'

'I was a dick, so I had another think. Maybe we could have a drink on neutral ground that might work okay.'

'Maybe. Not here though,' she said, checking Steve's departure. 'At the wine bar around the corner?'

'Lead the way.'

At the outside table, Roxie sat back, drew down her sunnies in the last of the sunshine for the day. A bottle of Aglianico red was on the table between them. 'I've enjoyed myself,' she said. 'Despite what you stood for.'

'We're human on the other side of the line.'

She smiled thinly at that. They'd kept off the differing opinions, it appeared by silent mutual consent. And he didn't look to be working too hard at being pleasant, either. Just seemed a natural guy. *Even so, nice people will still lie to your face.* 'We're poles apart in our philosophy.'

'I'm not trying to convince you to come to the dark side.'

'Isn't that exactly your job?'

Balfour sat his glass down on the table between them. 'I have a master's degree in business, specifically in mining and exploration. I understand the engineer's reports, the legal requirements of a government backed exploration. I know NOPSEMA back to front.'

Roxie held up a hand. 'I'm going cold on enjoying myself.'

He gave a laugh, nodded. 'Yeah, okay. What I'm trying to say is, maybe I could put all that knowledge and expertise into something that works for change.'

'Yeah right.' Her gaze narrowed. 'All those bloody massive companies could patent bio-fuels tomorrow. They probably have already, just to keep the technology quiet. Why wouldn't they start the rebuild to alternative fuel options? They'd win over the shareholders for generations to come.'

'Altruism doesn't pay. We're talking money here, and not the small change of a few hundred million bucks.'

A couple of glasses of red and Roxie wasn't exactly feeling patient. 'Look, right now, we just want the exploration and the drilling to stop. That's it. Bugger off oil and gas.'

'Naïve.'

'I don't have to remain polite.'

He sighed. 'Drilling won't stop in our lifetimes—even though they are working on it.' Was it a lie? He didn't know, but it was worth a shot to hold the peace.

Roxie reached over and poured each a share of the last of the bottle. 'You think they'll make it all their own idea then, once they figure out that this protecting the environment stuff might save their own arses?'

'That's what you lot want isn't it? Everyone running around barefoot, back to the horse and cart—us converted to clean and green and pristine. Go the Greens, et cetera.'

'Not the Greens Party. But if you're talking about the *greenies*, and the activists, they have their jobs, their roles in all of this. They keep the issues on the front lines, in the papers, on social media on the telly—deep sea oil exploration, the Taiji dolphin cruelty, and whale hunting, baby seal hunting and all our issues. But militancy won't change much, and bleating ideology won't help either. Education will. And it's a slow road.'

Balfour nodded. 'That's more my style. Education. I just don't see there's many good paying jobs in it.' He waited a beat, sat back, looked as if he was being—what? *Expansive?* 'What about yours? Job good?'

She shook her head. 'Thinking about quitting.' She didn't offer any more.

'Harder to get a good job if you quit before you find another one.'

Yeah, not expansive. Patronising. Sheesh. 'No kidding.' Roxie took another sip of wine. 'I don't need a high paying salary that bad, that I'd have to stay in a job I don't believe in.' She heard her own tone. Too late to retract it, she just slapped on a smile and stopped herself short. She was doing exactly what she was accusing him of—holding on to a job she no longer believed in. The uni wasn't for her. That job with du Pont and McKay—it wasn't for her. She wasn't going to change things by being anywhere near it. She knew it and knew it consciously. So who was she fooling? She was just hanging on to the money, too.

'I sleep at night.' He shot her a look. 'I like a high paying job and I don't need an excuse to have it. There's not a highly enough paid job in educating the world to make me want to change.'

'Is that so?' she said. He sounded smarmy. 'Thought you just said you'd look for one.'

He shrugged, seemed annoyed. He looked at his hands, leaned forward, elbows on his knees, and gave a lop-sided grin. 'Maybe I'll have another look. You never know.'

Now he was playing her. Fed up, Roxie drained her glass. 'You're right. I can't see you jumping ship.'

'I can't. I really need a safety net.'

'Must be a big deal to need that.'

'It is.' He finished his wine. 'Another drink?'

Shaking her head, Roxie stood up. 'I have to write up a few things, check in with the office.'

He got to his feet. 'I heard there's a boat going out tomorrow on a dolphin cruise. Wouldn't mind taking the fam.'

'Sure, come along if you want. It's open to anyone who pays. I'll make sure Jed doesn't bite.' When he held out his hand to shake hers, she took it, didn't linger. 'See you at the jetty tomorrow morning, then, eight o'clock,' she said.

Roxie left the wine bar and didn't look back. *An oil and gas guy on the survey boat tomorrow. Well, it's a free country. It wouldn't hurt to have him on board. He might get a clue.*

Deciding to take the stairs to her floor in the hotel and not the elevator—avoiding a meeting with Steve McKay in an enclosed space—she knew the first thing she'd do when she fired up her laptop. Resign. No more playing a game she was no good at. She was needed here, clear-headed, clear thinking, working at the very thing that kept her getting out of bed every morning.

She felt the flutters, felt energy ripple though her. There was a helluva lot she could put in place, a helluva lot needed doing. She'd get some sort of paying job here, no problem. She needn't waste her time playing footsies with some jerk who thought she was a fool.

Ten

Zeehund wobbled in the water. *Just like it's supposed to, but I wish it wouldn't.* Leonie had one foot on the boat, and the other on the wharf as she held on to Josh.

'I can get in on my own, Mum.'

'Of course, you can,' she said and maintained her grip on his arm. *I can't.* He propelled beyond her and stepped into the boat, leaving her grasp. He headed straight for Rob who stood at the helm, dodging the other fifteen or so passengers as he went. They'd wandered about the boat, windbreaker jackets zipped up, hats on heads tied under chins, aviator glasses on every face. Most had cameras about their necks, others had binoculars.

'Come on, Angie,' she said, trying to encourage her daughter on board.

Angie stood on the wharf, shaking her head, refusing to get on board. Overnight, it seemed she had retreated again.

Zeehund still wobbled on the buffeting little waves. Leonie was feeling slightly ridiculous and a little bit queasy. A stiff, intermittent breeze whipped her hair around, and the ends of it stung her eyes. All she could do was hope that the bits would fly back the other way. Her inner thighs were beginning to protest straddling the water between boat and wharf.

'Come on, sweetie,' she urged Angie. 'Just grab my hand and climb on board.'

Angie stood on the wharf not moving and beyond, Leonie spied Jed and Evie coming up behind her daughter.

'Hey, Angie,' Jed said, and stopped alongside the girl. Evie ducked around them and climbed on board. 'We're going to check if any of our friends from yesterday has decided to come back to the beach.' He looked at Leonie and nodded, kept talking to her daughter. 'And if so, we're gonna need a hand identifying them, and taking notes. Can you handle a pen and paper for me?'

Angie turned a little, being a bit braver. She stood only as high as his chest. Jed bobbed down to her. 'Could be that the dolphin mum from yesterday has got confused again. We don't want that.'

Leonie was beginning to get the *hang* of this, well, hanging between boat and jetty. She waited a couple of beats—a couple of waves—then saw Angie nod.

'Well, off you go with your mum and I'll be right behind you,' Jed said.

Flicking him a grateful glance, Leonie held her hand out again for Angie's cold, slim one. Tugging her daughter on board was easy, Angie seemed to float once she was past the wharf's edge. Leonie stepped onto the boat deck and Jed followed.

'Thanks.'

Jed nodded. He checked back over the wharf and up beyond the boardwalk to the carpark. 'Your brother still coming?'

Leonie had heard from Pete last night about the ruckus at the meeting yesterday. 'He organised it, so he must be.' She stood a moment wondering what to do. She was torn between wanting to get involved with the Dolphin Watch crew and seeing her daughter once again break through the shock of her father's death, and loyalty to her *forgot-my-nephew* brother.

'Ah. There he is.' Jed turned and yelled to Rob. 'Oil and gas guy's coming.'

Leonie looked beyond Jed and sure enough, Pete was jogging towards them on the boardwalk. He waved and she waved back. Last night can't have been that bad if he decided to turn up and come out on The Enemy's boat.

Then the woman with the mass of red curly hair paced alongside him. She took the lead a little and landed at the boat before him, hardly puffing at all.

The look on Pete's face said it all. So, this woman was the incentive behind her brother booking this trip.

'G'day. I'm Roxie Lockett,' the redhead said as she waited to come on board.

'Leonie Miller.'

A quick grip of hands and Roxie edged past Leonie, stalked past Evie and headed up to Rob at the wheel. Waiting for Pete, Leonie watched as Roxie casually slung an arm over Rob's shoulder and leaned in to scan the dashboard. *Are they just good friends?*

Pete stood at the boat. 'Well, I'm here.' He, too, glanced at the two people at the wheel. 'Anyone happy to see me?'

Leonie stepped back into the boat. 'At least you made it.'

He followed her. 'Might as well see how the other half lives.' He shoved hands in his pants' pockets, the long leg cargo's hems fell over hiking boots. Probably the only outdoorsy stuff he owned. He had on a new-looking thick polar fleece hoodie in dark blue, emblazoned with the Australis Island Dolphin Watch logo.

'Nice jumper,' she commented drily. 'You in disguise, mate?'

'It's a loan. Roxie got it for me.' He glanced again towards the wheel.

'Oh, really? Roxie? You think it'll work?'

'Very funny.' Pete wiped a hand over his face. 'We're friendly, that's all.'

'You're kidding me. She's for dolphins. And you're the oil and gas guy. She'll have your number, pal, not the other way around.'

'Always the smart-arse little sister, Leonie.'

'Smarter than you, it seems.'

Flynn loped on to the ramp, sunlight glinting in his close-cropped hair before he jammed on his cap. 'Am I the last one?'

Rob called from the wheel, 'Mate, untie us, wouldja?'

Flynn unwound the thick rope from the stanchion securing *Zeehund* to the wharf. He threw it into the boat, legged it over the rail and on to the deck. 'Ready to go, skipper.' He bent and coiled it, pushed it under a seat.

Rob gunned the motor and turned the wheel. *Zeehund* left her mooring, sleek and graceful, and headed out into the bay.

Passengers listened up as Rob welcomed them aboard. 'We need to get a bit further out towards our destination, folks, which is the pristine and calm Dashing Bay before we'll see a bit of action, but you never can tell how soon it might be. Our Citizen Scientists here—' he waved to a group of photographers and others all wearing the Dolphin Watch hoodie milling on either side of the boat, '—will record who we see in the water, and later that data will be transferred and the animals identified. We rely on this data to prove habitats and migration, and more.' He paused and spun the wheel a little to starboard. 'Now, just so you know, our beautiful Zeehund has twin jets, no dangerous propellers. Safe for our marine buddies. Most of the identifying marks we see on their dorsal fins are the result of prop damage, where boats approach at speed and the dolphins can't get out of the way quick enough.' There was a hush in the boat. 'Safe for us, too. We've also got life jackets on board for everyone.' He pushed the overhead mic arm out of his way and concentrated on what was in the distance.

Leonie saw that her son Josh was still by Rob's side, then she glanced around for Angie. Her daughter seemed to be sticking to Jed who pointed at different things on the boat as if he was explaining everything's function. How much she was taking in, Leonie couldn't tell. But the rapt expression on her face was a giveaway. Whatever Angie had been fearful of five minutes ago, had gone. Jed had made magic again. *Bless his socks if he'd been wearing any.* He brought Angie back to her and took off down the back of the boat.

Evie excused herself past Leonie and headed for a seat near the bow. She settled in, and pulled a camera out of her jacket, slung the strap around her neck and surveyed the water ahead through the lens.

Next thing, she turned and said something to Rob and he shouted, 'Starboard, about two o'clock.' He waved an arm, pointing over the right side, and turned the wheel. The boat powered down.

Heads swivelled. Cameras came up to eyes, phones on video thrust out at the ends of arms, passengers surged towards the starboard side of the boat.

That was quick. We're hardly out of the bay. Leonie gave Rob a grin when he spotted her, then she herded Angie towards the rail.

She heard his voice at the mic again. 'We've got a whole lot more lined up for you today. We're gonna see seals, and we're gonna see sea eagles and osprey. We might let you swim with these wild dolphins—bottlenoses, they are—in a shallow and protected area that will take your breath away. And just so you know—we know some of these animals have travelled at least a thousand kilometres, maybe a lot more than that. But what if you don't wanna get wet? That's okay, too. We got home-made treats for morning tea at a remote beach. We'll pass through a half a billion-year-old fossil bed, and then we'll cruise along white sandy beaches before we head back home. My idea of heaven, people.'

'Heaven,' Leonie heard Josh's boyish voice echo over the mic as he agreed with his new best friend.

Leonie smiled at that. It certainly looked as if her kids felt it was some kind of heaven. Although Angie still hadn't spoken today, her eyes shone as the dolphins played in the wake of the boat. Other animals frolicked starboard and port, some whipped across the bow and Leonie learned the true meaning of rubberneck. Turning around fully, she was taking in the number of dolphins in the pod when Angie squealed.

Heart failure—but Angie was leaning over the rail and pointing excitedly at a dolphin close by. Leonie grabbed her daughter's jacket. *Dear God, what if she'd leapt in?*

'Jed. Jed,' Angie squeaked, but he hadn't heard her. 'Jed. Jed.' She kept croaking his name and pointing over the rail.

Leonie huddled up behind her daughter and followed her finger. 'Is that—'

Pete slid up beside Leonie. 'What is it?'

'I think it's the dolphin Angie and I helped with yesterday.'

'It is her, it is her,' Angie yelled. 'It's Three Nicks.' The dolphin kept along Angie's side of the boat, lifted a little out of the water then plunged again for a dive, only to bob up again still in sync with Angie.

Sure enough, three notches in the fin. Leonie's mouth dropped open. Swore the dolphin's gaze was locked on to Angie somehow.

Jed was over in a second. He nudged Pete out of the way. 'That sure looks like our Three Nicks, doesn't it, Angie?'

And then the dolphin powered off. Leonie immediately felt Angie's energy drop.

Jed must have, too. 'Don't worry,' he said. 'If it's her she'll stay around for a bit. But she's got pod-work to do. She'll keep an eye on you, though.' He pushed off the rail, grinned at Leonie, stepped around Pete and left for Evie at the bow.

Angie pulled out of Leonie's huddle and went after him.

Pete laid a hand on his sister's arm. 'Let her go. She'll be fine with them.'

Leonie watched as Evie hooked her arm through Angie's, sandwiching her daughter between her and Jed. Evie pointed out to sea and Angie started to hop up and down.

'It's really amazing, Pete,' Leonie said. Rubbing a hand over her mouth, and then swiping at unbidden tears, she bumped shoulders with her brother. 'All the therapy, all the worry, the searching for answers, the guilt… And it takes a stranded dolphin to bring her out.'

'Nah, she was just ready.' Pete was watching the dolphin pod keep up with *Zeehund*, race ahead, double back.

Leonie shook her head. 'You didn't see her yesterday. It was as if something waved a magic wand over her. Like she woke up, just like that.'

Pete, still with his hands in his pockets and eyes on the dolphins, didn't look like he'd heard her. 'They're pretty used to this game, skimming along, scooting off,' he said.

Leonie followed his gaze. The animals were diving deep and would speed back to the surface and glide through the boat's waves. She tried again. 'You should have seen her—'

'It won't be what you think it is, Sis.' His tone was flat. He had heard her. 'It won't be the magic fix.'

'Why not? And how would you know? You weren't even there.'

'It's just a coincidence that she sparked up. Don't make out it was some sort of connection between Angie and Flipper.'

Leonie scoffed. 'Jeez. Flipper. How old *are* you?'

'Wondered that myself lately. Look, Sis, our Angie just needed a bit of time to come back, all by herself. Bit of fresh air, sand and sea, and all that.'

'Pete, there's a magic here. You just have to feel it.' She looked away as he gave a short laugh. She went on regardless. 'They say it has a spell. I know it, I felt it. So did Angie. Nothing on the mainland can compare to this. It has to be protected. Has to stay pristine.'

'The world needs oil, Sis. And some of it is five hundred and fifty ks that way buried deep under the water. What else do you think built this boat? Or is the stuff in those lifejackets, or in my shades?' He turned and pointed at his sunglasses. 'You've gone all wussy on me.'

Leonie watched Angie talking to Evie and Jed, waving her hands and jumping with glee when her dolphin surfaced for seconds here and there, to show off with leaps and splashes. It didn't really matter what had brought Angie back. All that mattered was if she was going to stay a while, and not retreat. But if dolphins had brought her back, then Leonie would make damned sure her daughter would be around them.

She glanced at her brother but didn't say anything. Maybe the time was right to let him off the hook. She wasn't a wuss.

He was watching Angie's dolphin dart back and forth, watched Angie try to keep up in the game. Pete had been generous. Too generous, taking in her and the kids and making sure they were all right. But she wouldn't let him do it forever.

Maybe the time is now. As soon as they got back to shore, she would check to see what rentals were available on the island. Check to see where she could enrol the kids for school. Check that she could find a job—she'd work at whatever was available. It was time to get back on her own feet. Terry was gone, and had been long gone from her life, if the truth be known. Not the kids' lives, of course. But her brother shouldn't have to pick up her pieces. Or Terry's. She appreciated his help—of course she did—but maybe now was the right time to go it alone.

She glanced at Pete again. He wasn't watching the dolphins now and didn't have his eye on Angie, either. His gaze was squarely on Roxie Lockett who was head to head with the skipper, Rob Carson. Leonie didn't miss the quick grin he gave her when Roxie lifted her gaze looking around. Roxie didn't grin back, barely glanced his way. Pete was fooling himself. *Shoe's on the other foot, bro.*

Pete swung his shoulders, his hand deep in his pockets. 'They're only friends, you reckon—Roxie and Rob?'

Gusts blew Leonie's hair, and salt stung her cheeks. The air smelled good, clean. She watched as the conversation at the wheel continued. Then Rob turned around and smiled directly at her. 'Yep. They're only friends.'

Eleven

Jed coiled the rope around the jetty stanchion after Flynn had tossed it off the boat. Evie stood with him as passengers disembarked, filed past, a thank-you and a see-ya-later from most of them.

Young Angie was with her mother and her brother. Jed had told her that he and Evie would catch up with them soon. They headed off along the jetty and into the carpark.

Evie tapped him on the shoulder. 'You should've kept up your skipper's licence. Get another boat and you and Rob could make a killing.'

'Off-season would do the killing,' Jed said, his eye on Roxie who was still on the boat, and talking to that Oil-and-Gas Guy. 'I don't need to be skipper. I just bank roll the thing. It's Rob's party.'

'Rob should buy it then,' Evie said.

'You know well as I do Rob can't buy it.'

'You don't have to bank roll him all his life, though.'

He flashed a look at her. 'He's an employee,' he said. 'Like you are.' He was quick to qualify when she bit her lip. 'I meant, that he has a job, like you, and the others. He wouldn't have a job if I got back in the skipper's seat.' *Shit*. He couldn't get back in the skipper's seat, didn't have the nerve yet. Maybe soon. And he didn't want Evie all possessive, either. She was a PA, nothing more. She just needed to look out for the business. 'I don't need to head up the company *and* drive the boat.'

She waited a moment, seemed to let go of whatever was bothering her. 'We still on for drinks?' She stepped closer.

'Sure,' but his gaze wasn't on Evie. He watched Roxie and that Balfour guy still talking as they made their way over to disembark.

He stopped them. 'You got a minute before you go, Roxie?'

Balfour said to her, 'Wine bar for another drink?'

'Maybe one.'

He lightly touched her on the arm before he left.

Jed felt his chest squeeze when he saw it. *Jesus*. Annoyed, he could do without Evie earwigging. 'Evie, do you mind?'

She tilted her head. 'I'll see you at the pub, then,' she said, all flouncy.

Roxie rolled her eyes as Evie left. 'Just tell her you're not interested, Jed. It's not fair on her.' She folded her arms.

'None of your business. Shut up.'

'Oh, that's so grown up. Typical of you. Head in the sand,' she said, and looked snaky as hell. 'So, what is it you want?'

Rob bounced past them. 'Catch you later. I'm having drinks then tea with Leonie.' He waved and took off at a run.

Flynn wandered up, staring after Rob. 'Joys of spring,' he commented drily as he finished up stashing life jackets. 'Good for him.' He stepped onto the jetty. 'See you up there for a drink?'

Jed looked about. *Shit. Anyone else coming off the boat?*

Roxie nodded at her brother, and called after him, 'And I need to talk to you about something.'

Flynn said, 'Sure, Sis,' and waved off as he followed Rob.

'What do you want, Jed?' Roxie asked again.

'What are you doin'?' He flicked his head towards the Oil-and-Gas Guy.

'Are you asking me what I think you're asking me?'

True to form, she'd fired right up. He snorted. 'So, has du Pont and his slimy mates got you trading off with oil and gas now? Is that part of your brief as a PA?'

'What?' She gave him the squint-eye.

'Maybe oil and gas are gonna fund R&D.'

'Oh, don't be ridiculous.'

Jed shrugged. 'Seem pretty cosy with that Pete Balfour guy.'

'Jed, too much weed, mate. You concentrate on Evie, okay?

Forget whatever it is you reckon you know about me.'

'I know a lot about you.'

'Maybe you did a while ago, but that was before you went crazy and all activist-warrior.' She sucked in a breath and her face was going red. 'I stopped thinking that you and I had anything in common long before you slugged that guy for setting up in opposition to you.'

'That wasn't the reason I slugged him. He had his hand on your—'

'No, he didn't. You just decided that was a good enough excuse. You got so caught up with Sea Shepherd, and then you went chasing down Japanese whalers, you made yourself sick over all of it. Couldn't work, couldn't drive the boat. Couldn't stop crying.'

Jed went quiet. Well, yeah, nah, not his best couple of months. He knew he hadn't looked after himself. Knew he'd burned out, burned right out. Had nothing left in his tank. Nervous breakdown, they said. Earlier, Roxie had tried to warn him. 'It's not the way to do it,' she'd raged at him. 'It's my way,' he'd said. And she'd walked off, saying, 'Then I'm not going down with you.'

'You let it get to you,' she said, exasperated.

'That was years ago,' he said. 'I was a youngster.'

'Three years ago. And you're only barely holding on now. You're letting all this business in the bight consume you again.'

'So it should, for all of us. But I'm fine.'

'You're not. You nearly blew it at the meeting with McKay and du Pont. McKay could press charges. And then with that oil and gas guy.'

'McKay yanks my chains. You're just playing their game, Roxie. This R&D mob, they got no heart. And Contour and their mates, the spill response mob, it's just the dollars for them. Just their jobs. You know there are better ways to do what they do.'

'I do know,' she snapped. 'I'm in there trying to make R&D

understand, trying to change the culture. I'll be doing things better, Jed. Differently. I'm not going to be that wired-up warrior anymore, getting people's backs up.'

'Keeping the focus, you mean.'

'And getting nowhere being a bloody martyr for the cause. That never did anyone any good. Didn't do you any good, or the dolphins, did it? I want good journos on our side, I want good media, not spin, not tabloid crap, and certainly not bolshy bloody flag-waving activists.'

'Then come back. Do it differently from here. We'll get funding. Easy.'

She threw her hands up in the air. 'I'd need to chase it down, hard. It won't be easy, and there won't be much of it. We need sponsors. And if I come back here, it won't be so you can think I'm okay with you, and how you do things, because I'm not. Do you get it? I'm not. I'll be doing everything very differently, Jed. Without your say so.'

A fiery streak roared up through his guts. 'By sleeping with an oil and gas guy now instead of the R&D guy?' he yelled and stabbed a thumb in Balfour's direction as heat popped sweat down his back. 'That's you doing it different? That's how you're gonna change things?'

Her jaw moved, her nostrils blew out, then pinched white. She glared.

That pulled him up. *Shit*. The heat in him dropped away from his guts, he went cold. It was the whole stink-eye from her now. He'd fucked up again. Put his foot right in it and now she was more fired up than he was, except she looked better at hanging on to it. Maybe. Whatever. He didn't like the look of it and stepped back a bit. That was the sensible thing to do.

'That's why I'm not going near you again, Jed Devereaux. Because you don't make sense. You're still so jealous, and for no reason,' she raged between her teeth.

'You got tickets on yourself, Roxanne.' He was jealous, but it would only be true if he *admitted* it to her.

'It's over between you and me, has been for ages,' she said, seething, and thrusted a finger at him. '*You* don't change. *You*. *Your* attitude. There are heaps of ways to be right, but you go into a mortal spin because according to you there's only *your* way. But you are so wrong about me, and you know how being wrong makes you feel.' With arms folded again, maybe so she wouldn't smack him into next week with a bloody left hook, she spun around and marched up the jetty.

He had to stop her. Apologise. He *had* changed—well, at least he could apologise these days. Was hard, but he could do it, a bit. 'Listen, Roxie—'

'Fuck off.'

'Oh, that's so grown up,' he called, imitating her, and got himself the middle-finger salute.

Jeez, Devereaux, that all went well.

Twelve

The kids had raspberry lemonades. Leonie would pay for that later at bedtime; they'd be crotchety and overloaded with sugar. Maybe a big run on the little beach in front of the hotel would do the trick. In the meantime, they were both on their iPads, sunk into the lounge chairs, feet dangling off the floor, and eyebrows puckered in concentration. At least while she waited for the agent to get back on the line there was peace.

The pub wasn't busy. Rob was at the bar talking to the waiter, getting a bottle of something white. She'd just said a glass, but he insisted on the bottle. He came back with two glasses and a pinot gris. He held it up for approval and she nodded.

'Yes, three bedrooms, and a yard,' she said when a voice came back over the line. 'Walking distance to the school. Good. Thanks. See you there tomorrow.'

'Ah, you called a real estate agent. That was quick,' Rob said.

She wondered what the look on his face meant. Sort of surprised, sort of hesitant. 'I can't rely on my brother forever. And after Angie coming out of her shell for the first time in months, it seems sensible to look into living here a while.'

'Yeah. Why not?' He poured and they picked up their glasses. 'Cheers.' They sipped the wine. 'Might be too soon. It's not easy living here.'

'Same as anywhere, I suppose.'

'Better if you've got a job.'

'I'll find something. Besides, if you got kids at school, you get to know people, you join the sports clubs, all that stuff. I know the drill. There'll be something.' She smiled at him. He was back-peddling, fast as he could, she could see it clear as day. He must be worried she was going to chase him. *No way* was she going to fall all over him if she decided to live here. He'd just seemed like a nice guy. Yeah, she was interested, but not if he was having second thoughts. *No way.* 'Besides, dolphins are here,' she said with a little shrug.

'They're in a few places,' he said, glancing up. 'Not only here.'

Holy hell. All right. 'Yeah, I know but this is so clean here, safe for the kids. That's all I care about—my kids and their happiness. It'll be fine.' She took another sip. 'Hey, nice wine.'

He looked at his wine. 'So what sort of job will you get?'

'Maybe at the supermarket, you know, something school hours. Maybe a job in a café.'

'Right.' He caught sight of something past her shoulder. 'Hey, Jed and Evie, over here.'

Despite herself, her heart sank a little. It might have been nice to get to know him, but if all he wanted was some short-term fling, and couldn't wait to be done with her, well, she couldn't be bothered. *Ah well.* No harm done. A nice day out—would have cost Pete a bomb, but he was good for it. She'd just have this glass and head back to the hotel room. Order a pizza for dinner, watch the telly. Kids would be fine with that. Pete would do his own thing. And as soon as she could, she'd contact Angie's psychologist and check for alternative programs they could access from here on the island. She put on her game face as Jed and Evie strolled over.

'Mind if we join you?' Jed asked.

'Go ahead,' Leonie said brightly. 'I won't be staying long. Going to find my brother for pizza.' She smiled at Jed then at Evie as if she didn't have a care in the world. Because she didn't.

*

Around the corner at the wine bar again, Pete waited for Roxie. Wasn't sure she'd turn up but then he watched as she had a quick word with her brother Flynn who'd hugged her then waved off her invitation. He made a point of nodding to Pete, saying, 'See you, mate.' Not everyone hated his guts, then.

'Enjoy the day?' Roxie asked him.

'Was great. Wouldn't mind doing it again sometime.'

She nodded. 'For sure. Or if those dolphins beach again, you can help us out there, too.' A waiter brought a bottle of red, opened it and poured two glasses. 'My shout this time,' Roxie said and waved her credit card over the mobile terminal the waiter carried.

'What did you decide to do?' he asked. 'Still quitting your job?'

'I gave notice half an hour ago. I'll be back here in two weeks. Flynn has a cottage here that he keeps for the occasional B&B. It's coming into the slow tourist season, reckon he wouldn't mind renting it to me full time.'

Pete was surprised. 'Back here? What'll you do?'

'For money? I've got a few contacts here and there. Know a few people. There's always something if you want work. I didn't think I would do it, could do it, but I'll be okay.'

He snorted. 'I wouldn't ditch my job.'

She took a breath. 'Yeah, whatever. It's just a job.'

'The environment doesn't pay, Roxie.'

'I'll do my bit here.' She lifted an eyebrow. 'If we don't have a healthy environment, nothing pays.'

Yeah, yada yada. 'Look, if it's not Contour Oil and Gas—and likely not—it'll be a smarter outfit. They're lining up and they've got real big money. Scandi money, the kind of money that can outwait Contour Oil and Gas. They've just watched NOPSEMA practice on my company, and they're laughing. They play a game better than anybody.'

Roxie tilted her head, lifted a shoulder. 'We'll fight on. Keep the noise level up. Be the terriers at their heels. We'll stop them.'

'It's not that simple.' He somehow knew he wouldn't win arguing the point. She was winding him up.

'It is,' she said, quietly stubborn. 'It just isn't easy.' She leaned back and took a good sip of wine, nodded in appreciation. 'You're happy on the Other Side.' She did air quotes with one hand. 'All that money.'

'I'm just staying with what I know, thanks, with the facts,' he said, abrupt. She was having a bloody go at him, all nice and polite.

She stood, gave a short laugh. 'You do that. We all do really, stay with what we know,' she said and screwed the cap back on the bottle. She took a big swallow from her glass and set it down. 'I'm off to catch the others. Thanks for giving up your holiday time to have a friendly chat with all of us.' She smiled a half smile that didn't reach her eyes. 'You needn't have, we got nothing new out of it.' She slid the bottle into her giant-sized tote bag and with a wave of her hand left him sitting there.

He didn't say anything, just watched her leave.

He'd stay with what he knew, all right. He'd stay with a big job for the money, for everything he'd known since leaving uni—the corporate world, the take-no-prisoners position. He wouldn't take a second look at people like Roxie Lockett, and he made no excuses for it. First because it was his life to do with whatever he wanted. Second because the greenie hicks were just time wasters. And third. *Uh yeah*, because his sister and the kids needed looking after.

Shit. I just put family last.

He took the last gulp of red. He thought a moment. Roxie's gaze had been on him till that last minute, those green eyes wide, a candid stare, daring him. In an instant he'd seen winter's nights here, the wind howling, the rain pelting, that firewood stove blazing, maybe a good red in hand again. And someone like her tucked in alongside him on a large settee. But he'd blinked and it had gone. She'd played him, having that drink. She'd probably seen right through him from the start. Wanted the last word.

You sorry bugger, Balfour. Get over yourself. Life would be better with someone by his side who thought like he did. Not like Roxie Lockett who was nothing to him.

His phone pinged a text message alert. It was from Leonie.

Meet at the pizza bar. Hurry up. Spoke to real estate agent. Got to

talk to you.

What the hell?

*

Jed thought Rob looked a bit strange when Leonie waved a cheery goodbye as she left the pub. He lifted his glass. 'Mate, something I said?'

Rob shook his head. 'Nah.'

Evie piped up. 'She was just going to get her brother and head for pizza, right?'

Jed's gaze was still on Rob. 'Thought you were interested in her.' The bloke had to have some fun soon, and that Leonie woman looked pretty keen.

'I dunno. I never want to get that interested.'

'You guys,' Evie said and huffed. 'Rob, she looked interested in you.'

He just shook his head again. 'Not going there, or anywhere else. It's not for me.'

'God, you're just like all the boys.' Evie gave a laugh. 'No commitment.'

She side-glanced Jed who didn't get it. *Commitment to what? What the fuck was she on about now?*

'Run and hide, hey?' she said to Rob.

'What else do you come to Australis for?' he snapped back, his face suddenly more contorted than usual.

She held up her hands. 'Okay, okay. Just teasing.' Miffed, she sat back in her seat.

'So, what's with this oil and gas guy?' Jed asked Rob, changing the subject before Evie could open her mouth again. Girl-shit always went over Jed's head.

'Who cares? They're all the same. If it's not him it'll be the next guy. They reckon it's coming no matter what we do and that we'll just have to get used to it.' Rob took a long swig of what was left in his glass.

'Nope. Will never get used to it. We keep fighting. I'm going to keep fighting.' Jed leaned over his beer. 'Just wish we could get all the data info logged quick enough to satisfy everyone, influence all these bastards.'

'Influence which bastards? R&D? The uni? Contour? NOPSEMA? The bloody heads-in-the-sand governments? Which?'

'All of the above. It's what they want. They want the data to support what we're petitioning for. At least there's an easy one for 'em straight up—they've legislated to slow down the stink boats in designated areas.'

'I know, I know.'

Jed scratched his head, pushed back a hank of his salt-stiffened hair. 'Something's gotta ensure the safety of our dolphins. People have to show them respect. It's not just talkin' about it that'll help, it's our solid data.'

'They're not gonna be convinced by us,' Rob said, holding up the bottle and checking for the dregs. 'You know, the fact that oil and gas are moving much faster than we are, that they *can* move much faster than us … What real hope have us little fellas got against all of them and all their money?'

Jed blinked. He wasn't giving up, but Rob's words, his *mate's* words sounded like he was giving up. He always thought Rob was a fighter. It didn't take much for his breath to stop, for the blood to pound in his ears. Emotion welled up and constricted his throat. *Dammit.* He squashed it down. Didn't want Roxie to be right. Again. *Breathe.*

'David and Goliath,' Evie said, and slowly nodded her head.

David and Goliath. Was Jed supposed to know what the fuck she was talking about? He didn't want to encourage her by asking the question. Instead, he said, 'I'm not giving up just because they're bigger'n us.'

'Exactly,' Evie said, like some wise old smart person.

Frowning but otherwise ignoring her, Jed took a swallow of beer. 'I'm gonna fight 'em every inch of the way until I've got nothin' left.' Evie went quiet and looked at Rob, who went quiet. *Well, that was a friggin' blessing.* 'We don't want any oil and gas exploration here. We don't want them destroying a pristine wilderness habitat.' Jed rolled out his spiel and he could feel a pressure in his chest again. He was getting mad. Evie laid a hand on his arm but he shrugged it off. 'And we don't want those bastards darting our animals. I'm gonna go see that McKay guy, let him know what's what.' He got to his feet.

'Mate,' Rob said. 'We're fighting on too many fronts. Flynn's up to his neck on our north coast in the Jones Bay saga with the timber mob and the deep water port. It won't help to go for McKay.'

Jed felt his lip curl. 'Given up already, have you, boyo?'

Rob stood, his mouth a taut line. '*Zeehund* needs maintenance now, *boyo*. That will help, not you runnin' off getting beat up. You comin' or not?' he asked. 'At least I won't punch your lights out like that McKay guy will. He'll be waiting for you.'

Evie put down her empty stubbie of beer. 'We need to get the survey data logged before we get too many beers under our belt here,' she said. 'Come on, back to the shed. At least there are beers there.' She marched off. 'Come *on*,' she ordered over her shoulder. 'And pinch your nose, Jed. Your nostrils are flapping.' Then she wrenched open the door and shut it behind her.

Jed rubbed a hand over his nose and chin. He needed to calm himself. He needed to remember how to disarm.

Roxie met them as Jed and Rob blundered out the door behind Evie. 'I was just coming to get you all for a drink,' she said. She held the wine bottle to show them.

'We're goin' to the shed.' Jed cut her off, glaring, and strode off.

Rob waited a moment with her. 'I gotta check over the boat. Then we gotta log the data. Berta and Tomas will be there, firing up the computers already.'

'Good. I'll come help.'

'Won't be a help, Rox, if you and Jed get into a brawl.'

She blew out a breath. 'Walk with me,' she said and poked Rob on the shoulder. They headed away from the pub and down the road to the wharf and Jed's shed. 'I'm coming back to the island. I've quit. I'm going to explore ways to fund what we do here, to keep the ball rolling.'

Rob started a happy laugh, then checked himself. 'Yeah, but—you know Jed.'

'We have to keep Jed under control. If we're going to do this—if I'm coming back to do this, he needs to be stable.'

'Good luck with that.'

Roxie turned to him. 'I won't be doing it on my own, Rob. Not again. His emotional issues are too much for me, and not my problem. If I go down this track, he has to be contained. That means all of you have to help—Evie, Berta and Tomas, Flynn, you.'

Rob's eyes popped. 'You don't think we haven't been doing that while you've been away?'

She ignored that. 'Contain him, otherwise he'll ruin it.'

'Otherwise he'll kill himself, you mean. Blow out again.'

'Yeah, there's that too,' she said, looked away and let go a long sigh.

Rob thrust his hands in his pockets. 'He's never got over you, Roxie.'

'That's too bad.' And she meant it. Even if, when she heard herself say it, it cut her like a knife. *No. No going back, not to that.* 'But life goes on.'

'You got something goin' on with the oil and gas guy?'

She snorted. 'God, no, and you do *not* think that. He talks oil and gas and his high-falutin' credentials then he talks taking a job with spill management as if he's taking some sort of high road.'

Rob kept up with her. 'Yeah?'

'He's snotty. He's defensive, but I reckon he'd jump ship faster than a rat. Tried to keep the oil spill response thing downplayed. Why have a such a big response centre if there's not gonna be a big spill? Thinks I didn't have a clue. And,' she said and gave him a sideways look. 'Thinks he got away with it.' She shoved open the shed door. 'Has he got another think coming.'

Berta and Tomas hovered over the computers and the laptops. Another couple were already there, too, Sue and John, peering at the pages. Jed was behind Evie, concentrating on her screen.

A large plate of lamingtons sat in their squat tower in the middle of the boardroom table.

Jed looked up at her a moment, then dropped his gaze back to the monitor. Evie was in the chair keying in the survey results. She flicked Roxie a smirk and settled in, while Jed continued to peer over her shoulder.

Roxie's lip started to curl, but she turned away before anyone saw her do an eye-roll. Rob pushed past her to grab a set of keys. 'I'll input a few when I get back. Need to look over the boat. Coming, Jed?'

Jed nodded at Rob. 'Let's get on with it, people. Get this data underway.' Then he met Roxie's stare. 'We're not gonna let them win, not any of them. Not R&D, not oil and gas. We're not goin' away. And we're building up our people, getting' more on their boards out into the water when we protest. We're gettin' more people on the sand for when the drones fly over from the mainland newsrooms—'

Roxie called over. 'Well, make sure you get all those wonderful people to write their submission, too, Jed, that'll help make a difference. One that's tangible, one that can be recorded.'

'They can't all do that, can't all handle computers and big words and shit.'

Eyebrows raised, Roxie realised that would be another job for her. 'They don't have to. Just get them in to see me each time we need to submit. Those drillers reckon if they get enough opposition they'll withdraw. We'll see about that. We'll keep hammering until we get it done. You'll see. The next mob will have changed their stance and procedures based on information we've provided.' She waved her hand at the rows of computers. 'We have expectations of them now. They have to change. It's just not all going to be only your way.'

Glaring at her, Jed said, 'I'll fight 'em my way 'til it kills me.' He headed for the door.

'Be my guest.'

Rob swiped up two lamingtons and pushed one at him as he strode past. 'Here, Jed, eat. Can't have it killin' you on an empty stomach,' he said and turned and gave Roxie a wink before following Jed outside.

She put her hands to her face and rubbed vigorously. She sat down at a computer, grabbed up a heap of survey papers, studied the pics.

As she clicked open the data pages on the screen, she knew they'd all fight on, each in their own way. They'd fight the good fight. They'd get more people on side, fight to kill off this exploration and drilling. The fight for a future safe environment would continue for the animals in the sea, for the people who guarded them, and for the livelihoods that relied on a clean ocean. There was nothing else *to* do. She believed it.

Pete Balfour stared at his laptop. Blank. He'd just pressed 'send', submitting his CV to the oil spill mob. A ping sounded, distracting him. A text message had dropped into his phone.

NOPSEMA denied our application. Company restructure meeting Monday 8th. Your presence required. Leave revoked.

Well, we all know what that means, Pete thought, and opened his draft resignation letter. He'd finish it now. He'd put in a long notice, six maybe eight weeks. If another job came up in the meantime, he'd take it and cut his losses at Contour. He'd wing it, he'd be fine. Leonie and the kids would be fine over here, he'd make sure of it.

He knew Contour Oil and Gas would not submit to NOPSEMA again. His job with them was done. But if the spill centre didn't want him, he'd apply to the big Scandi company. Wouldn't mind joining its ranks.

Outside, Jed was heading to the wharf chewing a mouthful of lamington when his phone pinged. He checked it and nearly choked. He whooped, coughing and spluttering and danced towards the boat, grabbing Rob in a half-Nelson.

'What—*what*?' Rob gurgled.

Jed thrust his phone in front of his eyes. 'It's from Flynn. We fight on, old mate,' he cried. 'There'll be others, but we beat this bastard. They'll never win.'

Contour Oil and Gas no go. NOPSEMA denied application.

Jed took off down the jetty.

Rob knew they hadn't beat Contour—Contour had defeated themselves, bloody bunch of cowboys. But it didn't matter. The next mob, slick-talkin' and moneyed up would have a go. They'd be bigger. Better at it. Sooner or later, one of them would win. But right now all he had to do was catch up with Jed as he headed towards their beloved boat.

In the distance, a pod of dolphins cavorted. Jed and Rob skipped and jumped like little kids down the wharf past Zeehund, whooping some more, and waving at the leaping animals, who were happy at the outcome of course, but took no notice.

Roxie was keying in data when her phone pinged an alert. Snatching it up to read the text message from her brother Flynn, she smiled, and tears popped. She thumped a fist over her heart, hissing, 'Yes.' Other alerts were sounding around the shed, and the cries of delight echoed her own.

Evie rushed over and hugged her. *That's a bit much, but forgiven.* Pushing her off with a smile towards Berta and Tomas,

Roxie checked Flynn's message again.

NOPSEMA denied application. Contour Oil and Gas submission dead in the water. Pardon the pun. Save the red, kiddo. I'm on my way with the champers. Next – Save Jones Bay!

About the author

Darry Fraser is a published author with HarperCollins.
She lives and works on the beautiful Kangaroo Island off the coast of South Australia.

www.darryfraser.com

www.ingramcontent.com/pod-product-compliance
Lightning Source LLC
Chambersburg PA
CBHW030448300426
44112CB00009B/1215